Me, Madam

Me, Madam

Peace Corps
Letters from Nigeria
1961–1963

Dorothy Crews Herzberg
Peace Corps Volunteer

Arc Light Books
Berkeley, California

Me, Madam: Peace Corps Letters from Nigeria, 1961–1963

Copyright © 2014 by Dorothy Crews Herzberg. All rights reserved. Except for use in a review, no portion of this book may be reproduced—mechanically, electronically, or by any other means, including photocopying—without written permission from the publisher.

Arc Light Books' publications are available at a discount when purchased in bulk. Special editions or book excerpts can also be created to specification. Contact: publisher@ArcLightBooks.com

---

Crews Herzberg, Dorothy, 1935–
Me, Madam: Peace Corps Letters from Nigeria, 1961–1963
   / Dorothy Crews Herzberg

ISBN: 978-1-939353-11-5

Published by
Arc Light Books
Berkeley, California

publisher@arclightbooks.com

www.arclightbooks.com

Cover and book design by Jan Camp

Back cover photos:
   Top row: Dorothy with Sargent Shriver, 1991
             The well-baby contest, 1963
   Middle: Dorothy with a neighbor in Nigeria, 1962
   Bottom: Father McGlade meeting the bishop, 1963

For
 Samuel,
  Laura,
   Daniel,
    and
     Hershel

Acknowledgments

I could not have pulled together these letters (written fifty years ago) and the narrative without the help of my writing groups. The group led by Beth Glick-Rieman and Lynn Hammond gave me confidence to keep going as we shared our stories every week for the past two years. My memoir group listened patiently to the letters and my ideas. It was important to read pages aloud to understand how they sounded to others. Thank you, Helen Burke, Kathy Bernhart, Charlotte Gray, Susan Kurjiaka, Jane Hirada, Nora Wagner, and Elizabeth Hutchins.

Many thanks to Beth Jerde, Helena Knox, and Kit Hewitt for reading the manuscript and noting corrections; to my husband Douglas Frew who patiently endured my stumbling on the computer; to my amazing book designer Jan Camp who went beyond professional expertise, bringing a sense of humor and delight to the story as it unfolded; and to Jessica Sevey for copyediting.

Contents

Author's Note	1
Training at UCLA	5
The Marjorie Michelmore Incident	8
Home Stay	10
My Assignment Begins	13
Teaching in Nigeria	20
Queen's College, Enugu	25
The Census	39
St. Teresa's College, Nsukka	45
Settling In	47
Father Desmond McGlade	59
Duodecimals	65
Sewing Projects	75
University of Nigeria, Nsukka	83
Perspectives on Nigerian History	83
Student Riots: University of Nigeria, Nsukka	92
Trip to Ivory Coast	100
January 1963 to August 1963	108
Toys from America Well-Baby Clinic	110
Final Word	139
Student Essays	147
Newspaper Clippings	151
List of Letters and Student Essays	158
About the Author	161

Mrs. Floyd H. Crews and her daughter Dorothy, before going to Nigeria

Dorothy's Father, Floyd H. Crews,
was a patent attorney in New York City

Author's Note

In 1986 over 5,000 returned Peace Corps volunteers gathered in Washington DC to commemorate the twenty-fifth anniversary of the Peace Corps. At a luncheon, in the Senate office building for the first 400 volunteers, Sargent Shriver, who had been the first director of the Peace Corps, told us that we were sent to Nigeria before the Peace Corps had actually been approved by Congress. The best argument the Peace Corps proponents had was that there were already four hundred volunteers overseas.

Senator Ted Kennedy told us that his brother, President John F. Kennedy, considered the Peace Corps the best thing his administration had achieved. He said his brother would have been at the luncheon to speak to us if he had been living. It was quite a moment.

While serving in the Peace Corps in Nigeria from 1961–1963, I wrote 100 letters home. My parents enjoyed the letters as a chronicle of my amazing two-years assignment. My father photocopied every single one and presented me with the originals and copies carefully preserved.

The letters are the basis of this book. Over the years I have often thought of putting them together, but could not envision how to do it. Rereading the letters in 2012, I found them so fresh and rich in detail that I was struck with a sense of urgency. I knew I had to present them somehow as they were originally written. My immediate reactions, opinions, and descriptions of events stand just as they were penned in the 1960s. I have added little contextual narrative so as not to intrude on the spontaneity of the letters.

This book is written chronologically, following the process of entering the Peace Corps in 1961, completing the training, and then working for the next two years.

When I entered the Peace Corps the idea of sending young Americans to work in developing countries was a new concept for the U.S. government. Nonprofit groups such as the American Friends Service Committee (AFSC) had sent volunteers to live in villages in Mexico for over thirty years. The Peace Corps invited countries in need to request volunteers to work in their schools or on projects. Jobs and housing had to be provided by the host country. Nigeria was one of the first to respond. Americans were skeptical. What possible contribution could young, naive, inexperienced Americans make? There were also concerns for the health and safety of volunteer abroad.

My initial assignment was to Queens College, Enugu in the Eastern Region of Nigeria. Secondary schools were called colleges. Queens College was a government school, the responsibility of the Minister of Education. In the Northern Region all secondary schools were run by the government. In the Western and Eastern Regions most secondary schools were run by missionaries. All secondary schools were boarding schools and the students generally came from surrounding villages.

The staff at Queens College included British women, wives of Nigerians, and one Nigerian woman. A British wife, Jill Eyoma, became my special friend. She had met her husband when they were both students at the University of Edinburgh. While she was raising two children, he was then studying for his PhD in Sweden. Jill died in 1962 from complications following surgery and it was devastating for me. I gave my daughter the middle name of Jill.

The curriculum followed at Queens College was the same as that offered to a student in England. This was done with the intention of making the degrees comparable, but it was particularly difficult to make history and English relevant. In the English literature class that I taught at Queens College, we read novels, plays, and poetry. There were numerous references that no student in Africa had experienced.

For example: autumn, spring, Christmas trees, clothing such as scarfs and boots, sports such as skiing and skating, and amusements such as circuses and carnivals, to mention a few.

My experiences in Nigeria involved much more than teaching. I also had one thousand books sent to Queen's College, Enugu from a charitable organization in the U.S. Being in Enugu, then the capital of the Eastern Region, provided chances for me to take students to watch sessions of the House of Assembly. There were opportunities to meet politicians and visiting expatriates such as Edward R. Murrow, and experience the nightlife during which I learned to dance the *highlife*, an urban style of dance that originated in Ghana.

While in the Peace Corps I married Hershel Herzberg. He was a volunteer with the first Nigerian group that had trained at Harvard and Ibadan. Hershel taught History at St. Teresa's College in Nsukka. I asked him recently about the curriculum. He covered the development of western civilization from 1066 to 1688. This included the Renaissance and Reformation, slavery, particularly as the West Coast of Africa was called the Slave Coast, and the travels of Columbus and the New World. It left out Asia and South America, any mention of the ancient kingdoms of Mali and others in Africa, and anything after the seventeenth century.

I moved to his compound in Nsukka, which was north of Enugu and deep in the tropical rain forest—the bush. It was totally different from Enugu. I found that in a tropical climate it was important to stay productive, to keep active. Every day after my classes, I drove into the bush and developed sewing projects in five villages. Since these went from June 1962 to June 1963, they overlap chronologically with other events, and I group together the excerpts describing the sewing projects.

There was a well-baby clinic in Nsukka where toys from America were distributed. In a tropical climate it is very difficult to stay healthy as insects, bacteria, and disease thrive. Virtually everyone got malaria. Babies were nursed for six to nine months. Then they would crawl or walk around the family compound, making it difficult, if not impossible, to keep them healthy. In the clinic nurses examined the babies and rewarded the healthiest as a way of rewarding the mothers.

In September 1962 I began teaching French at the University of Nigeria, Nsukka. The university was founded in 1955 and formally opened on October 7, 1960. It attempted to blend British and American curriculums. The British faculty would say:

"Journalism! That isn't a subject! You Americans are so funny."

"Teaching business administration in a university? What is that?"

Students followed the European tradition of taking a comprehensive exam in their major at the end of their senior year.

Hershel wrote letters to my parents. Neither of us realized how many he had written until I started compiling this book. I have included them just as he wrote them.

The details in our letters reveal the experience of what daily life was like. Our wedding and honeymoon, and subsequent struggle to establish a household, give some perspective. On our honeymoon we went to Dahomey, which is now the country of Benin.

Living on a school compound and teaching at the university gave me a rich and diverse experience of Nigeria. Since no one had telephones, televisions, or even radios, visiting each other for tea or dinner were the predominant sources of entertainment. Sitting after dinner and watching the rain from our little porch was always interesting, as the lightning was dramatic. I described this in my letters.

I hope I have conveyed what Nigeria was like immediately after independence, struggling to create a new democracy, absorbing advice from everywhere, and bursting with energy and pride.

Training at UCLA

The exam began at 8:30 a.m. I slipped into the only available seat at 8:29. Though the test was mostly general knowledge, I understood what lay ahead. I knew I wanted to be a teacher. But I wanted experience teaching abroad before settling down to an assignment in the United States. So I was ready for the exam and the Peace Corps.

With some rewarding experiences behind me, I knew the Peace Corps would be right for me. I had worked for the Fresh Air Fund for four summers. We took kids from Harlem to camps for ten days. First I worked as a counselor, then as a program director, and then as a director of one of the camps.

Another summer after college I worked with the American Friends Service Committee (AFSC) in a village in Mexico. We developed crafts projects, and organized recreation in the local school. We relied on our own resourcefulness and used the talents of our group. Now, with the Peace Corps, the government was going to emulate what the AFSC had been doing. During training I received a questionnaire from the Peace Corps asking for advice based on my experience with the AFSC.

In September of 1961 fifty of us reported to the University of California, Los Angeles (UCLA) for training to teach in secondary schools in Nigeria.

From September to December 1961 we had classes from 8:00 a.m. to 10:00 p.m. Most were held in a chemistry lab on campus, until we arrived one morning to find that the building had blown up from some neglected chemistry experiment. We met somewhere else.

Our days started with physical education, which consisted of sets of ten push-ups, ten sit-ups, and several other exercises. We repeated each set a few times. The boys learned to play soccer, as it was the popular sport in Nigeria.

We had language classes in Igbo, Yoruba, and Hausa, which were taught by Nigerians, some brought from Nigeria, as there were no instructors of these languages on the faculty. African languages are tonal, which meant that the sequence of tones conveyed different meanings. Very few of us, if any, mastered them. I did not. Also, there are several different dialects of Igbo so that villages a few miles apart had difficulty communicating. English was the official language since Nigeria had been an English colony for a hundred years, ending in 1960. All secondary schools where we would be going were taught in English.

We had lectures in Nigerian history, U.S. history, education, literature, and tropical medicine. Tropical medicine was graphic with slides of malaria, filariasis, schistosomiasis, hepatitis, dysentery, worms, syphilis, protein deficiency, etc. We received twelve different shots. We did practice teaching in the public schools. We saw psychiatrists, counselors, and dentists. We learned first aid and cardiopulmonary resuscitation (CPR).

Two young Nigerian writers, Chinua Achebe and Wole Soyinka, spoke about Nigeria and Nigerian literature. We had the privilege of meeting them before the rest of the world became acquainted with their work. In 1986 Wole Soyinka went on to win the Nobel Prize in Literature. However, Chinua Achebe is often recognized as being the most influential writer in Nigerian and African Literature.

One day on the way to practice teaching we had a car accident. Another day it was raining so hard the roads flooded. Another day there was a fire in the San Bernardino Mountains which encircled the university. From the rooftop of a university building we watched the fire jump from mansion to mansion in the hills.

During the next two years none of us experienced floods, fires, accidents, or explosions. But our training had prepared us.

UCLA EDUCATOR

SCHOOL OF EDUCATION • UNIVERSITY OF CALIFORNIA • LOS ANGELES

Volume 4   November, 1961

Foreground: Left to right, Anthony Fanniano, Dorothy Crews, and S. D. Awokoya, Chief Federal Education Adviser. Back row: Left to right; Peter Brigham, Joyce Carlson, Virginia Eck, Lillian Miles, Roberta Goodrich, and I. Mboto, Inspector of Teacher Training, Eastern Region. Mr. Awokoya and Mr. Mboto were among five Nigerian educational officials interviewing trainees at UCLA recently, in order to facilitate the individual assignment of the Peace Corps teachers in Nigeria.

PEACE CORPS PROGRAM OUTLINED

The UCLA program for Peace Corps volunteers got under way September 20 with 49 candidates reporting for training. The Los Angeles campus was one of nine university centers selected to prepare Peace Corps members for duties in underdeveloped countries. The group in training at UCLA will be assigned to instruct in the secondary schools of Nigeria in subjects ranging from Latin to vocational agriculture.

The major emphasis of the ten week program for the trainees will be on developing background knowledge of Africa and of Nigeria in particular. A full program of sixty or more hours of instruction and other activities is planned. Instruction for the candidates will include 120 hours of Nigerian studies, including geography, history, economics, political administration, anthropology, and social problems; 75 hours of education, including both comparative education and practice teaching; 50 hours of American studies, ranging over political, constitutional, and social subjects in both domestic and international settings; 60 hours of language orientation; 53 hours of health instruction; and 60 hours of physical conditioning.

Faculty for the project will be drawn from various departments and schools of the University. Dr. Wendell P. Jones, School of Education, has been named director of studies for the UCLA program, and Dr. Elwin V. Svenson of University Extension will be project administrator. They will be assisted by a committee of Dean Howard E. Wilson of the School of Education; Dr. Jesse A. Bond, professor of education; Dr. James S. Coleman, director of the African Studies Center; Dr. Benjamin E. Thomas, associate professor of Geography; Dr. Abbott Kaplan, Associate Dean of University Extension; and Dr. Charles E. Young, assistant to the Chancellor.

The Marjorie Michelmore Incident

Marjorie Michelmore was a volunteer in Peace Corps 1, training at Harvard as well as at the University of Ibadan in Nigeria. She was in Ibadan when this incident happened while I was at UCLA.

Marjorie had written a postcard home in which she described life in Nigeria. She accidentally dropped the postcard and a Nigerian student found it. Instead of mailing it or throwing it away, he realized it could create some excitement. Marjorie's postcard was copied and circulated around campus. Her description of Nigerian life was not of a beautiful, perfect paradise, and it was interpreted to imply that the Peace Corps had some malicious purpose. It angered some people.

At UCLA where we were training, we read the stories in newspapers and on covers of magazines and waited. People arrived from Washington to tell us that we may not be going. No one really knew what to do since the Peace Corps was so new and had no track record. TV, radio, and newspapers whipped up the story until it seemed almost possible that the Peace Corps would die before it had even been born.

Marjorie was sent home. The rest of the individuals in her group were not sent to their schools, but were held at Ibadan waiting for us to arrive.

We went.

In Nigeria I found that only politicians and some educated people had heard of Marjorie. None of the chiefs and ministers I met in Lagos or Enugu were very concerned. We were told to go into the bush to see how the villagers lived. We were welcomed everywhere. The postcard incident was forgotten.

Peace Corps Sends 39 More To Nigeria

R. Sargent Shriver, Director of the Peace Corps, asked a group of thirty-nine Peace Corps members yesterday, before their departure for Lagos, Nigeria, to be "sympathetic to the mistakes we have made." He made clear that the Corps members were expected to be "prudent, wise and circumspect."

Mr. Shriver addressed the group, all high school teachers, in the Pan American World Airways Terminal at Idlewild prior to their departure for Nigeria via chartered airliner. He said some mistakes had been made in administration and in training but these had been corrected.

He noted that the "postcard incident had not caused the end of the Peace Corps, as some critics had predicted. He referred to a postcard written by Marjorie Michelmore, of Foxboro, Mass., which commented on Nigerian living conditions and created a furore there when it became public.

"On the contrary, Nigeria continues to ask for more Peace Corps members, he said. The airport group brings the number of volunteers in Nigeria to 110. The country has requested 365.

Home Stay

The last two weeks at home before meeting at the airport were important.

I had a wisdom tooth pulled and I bought a little Minolta camera and a portable Olivetti typewriter. I also contacted a project called Operation Bookshelf that some volunteers were developing and arranged eventually for some one thousand books to be sent to me in Nigeria. There were Christmas parties in the neighborhood where I was asked repeatedly *why* I was going to Nigeria with the Peace Corps. No one could imagine making such a decision.

One night before I was to leave, my father got out a map of Africa—the only one he could find—and spread it out on the dining room table. "Now where exactly are you going?" he wondered.

I pointed to West Africa on the map. West Africa was covered with a big white blob. Over it had said, "White Man's Burden." I told him he had to get a new map. This one was out of date.

At the airport the next day my parents met Sargent Shriver and other Peace Corps volunteers (PCVs). I was not to see my parents again for two years.

Dorothy and other Peace Corps personnel leave for Nigeria in 1961

Peace Corps training group at UCLA, 1961

PEACE CORPS

WASHINGTON

OFFICE OF
THE DIRECTOR

Dear Dorothy,

    I am delighted that the schedule of your Peace Corps training affords you the opportunity to spend Christmas at home. But I hope that you will take advantage of your leave to reassess your purpose in joining the Peace Corps, and to reaffirm your dedication to the job which faces you.

    Nowhere is the spirit of the Peace Corps better expressed than in the spirit of the traditional American Christmas. With that thought in mind, then, please accept my best wishes for a very happy and a very Merry Christmas.

Sincerely,

Sargent Shriver

Sargent Shriver

December 15, 1961

My Assignment Begins

Letter of January 4, 1962

Dear Folks,

We have been on a train since Tuesday. We've been to Abeokuta, Kaduna, then south across the Benue River, and to Enugu at last! The countryside was much like Arizona and the southwestern United States—growing drier with scarcer vegetation as we went further from the equator. The trees reminded me of African sculpture, twisted with awkward grace like their sculpture. The train stopped often for water, passengers, and various obscure reasons. At each stop the people came running out of the tiny villages to greet us and sell us fruit and have their pictures taken. We played football along the tracks and delighted them with Polaroid pictures at one stop. At another, some of the kids wandered into the village for awhile.

We are all looking forward to seeing our villages at last and settling into our schools. Enugu is absolutely delightful, nestled in a valley between rolling hills. The city is of no historic importance, chiefly significant for its coal industry. It is the capital of the Eastern Region and as such, enjoys a bustling traffic of people, but retains a human-size quality. We were met at the station and photographed, loaded into a truck, and taken to the Nigerian Institute of Technology, where we have rooms and will be staying for a week. It is beautiful with tennis courts, a huge campus, and on the next hill right out of my window is Queens College! I called the headmistress this afternoon. I suspect she is Irish Catholic as the Eastern Region is predominantly Catholic. I will meet her and see the school tomorrow morning. We have eaten, washed, and scrubbed. And just now three of the most lovely sights in the world arrived—a trunk, a carton, and a suitcase. Wonder of wonders—undamaged!

In Lagos my last evening was a chief who had studied at Harvard that someone had suggested I contact. Well, he is absolutely charming and brilliant. He is the manager of the national press and several other things very important and popular in federal realms. He showed me Lagos and took me to a party where I met several other chiefs, all lawyers and doctors now, and all very jolly. One of them named Louis came to see us off at the station. He is an optometrist in town and quite delighted to meet all seventy-six of us and astonished at what we were doing. He says he will fly to Enugu to see us. It is only two hours by plane but three days by train. Anyway Chief D is wonderful and I will surely see him again. I wandered into a bookstore the next day and found a book written by him when he was at Harvard! I must read it right away!

My impressions of Africa so far are: hot, colorful, exciting! The people are friendly and eager to meet us. We've been welcomed everywhere. Everywhere too, we have seen buildings going up. We met three or four members of the Peace Corps group in Ghana. They spent their vacation visiting Nigeria. They have been teaching for four months already. They were overwhelmed by Nigeria and said its potential is infinitely greater than Ghana's! They were impressed with the electrification of so many towns and cities in Nigeria, by the diversity of agriculture and industry, and the size of the country. It seems undeniable that Nigeria will be the leading country in Africa in less than five years.

We are going, so I understand, to Nsukka on Sunday. It is a day's drive from Enugu and thirty to forty Peace Corps volunteers are stationed there teaching at the University of Nigeria, Nsukka. I suppose they want us to meet them.

I have taken pictures of the whole trip so far and I think I will send the two rolls home in a registered mail envelope. My little Japanese camera takes forty pictures on 35mm film made for twenty exposures. So on each roll there should be about forty pictures. They might take three weeks to reach you. I would love to know how they came out, as I have never used this camera before. I think I will buy film here. It comes with a little bag to ship it to England and I want to see how this works.

Love,
Dot

Letter of January 9, 1962

Dear Folks,

Well it's all settled. I'm to live with Miss Penny for a week to have time to purchase dishes and whatever, and then move into Miss Hernshaw's house for a month—it is only vacant until she returns. School starts the 26th of January. I may stay there until the end of February, actually, until my permanent house is vacant. One of the staff has asked for maternity leave so her house is mine. It has a coal stove and fridge, and is probably quite comfortable. I haven't actually seen it yet. So, I will be at Queen's School, Enugu after all. I took a ride with my headmistress and her husband past the coal mines. Their houseguest was an English woman. She exclaimed about the "wretched Igbo," "Why don't they tell these people to dress themselves?" She insisted on leaping through the woods with binoculars to examine all the birds she could find.

Our visit to Nsukka was most fascinating. The university is breathtaking—huge modern streamlined buildings, unfinished as yet and half empty. There was a stadium for thirty-five thousand people—they cannot possibly fill it with the student body they have now. The whole place is only three years old. I finished a roll of film and will send it to you. You won't believe the buildings—they are better facilities than most schools in the U.S. The administrative staff, including the deans and president are from Michigan State. Thirty Peace Corps volunteers are teachers but the majority of the staff is Nigerian. There are all kinds of conflicts and turmoil over whether to follow the American or British model. The files aren't completed, classes aren't programmed, rooms aren't assigned, and the university opened today. Everyone is learning a lot about how a university is put together. It is Zik's dream and his summer palace is behind it. (Zik is Nnamdi Azikiwe, president of Nigeria and chancellor of the university.)

We had a talk by a police officer this morning in which we learned that we need licenses for our radios. Everything is growing very rapidly—almost more than the economy or the population can absorb.

I will be dependent on the rest of the staff for transport for the moment. Congress is under pressure to provide us with something—the Ghana group have jeeps. Our headmistresses and headmasters are being asked to write letters. As usual, in Africa things will probably work out in time.

Love,
Dot

ADDRESS OFFICIAL COMMUNICATIONS TO
THE SECRETARY OF STATE
WASHINGTON 25, D.C.

DEPARTMENT OF STATE
WASHINGTON

JAN 1 1 1962

Dear Miss Crews:

Congratulations on your assignment to Nigeria as a Peace Corps volunteer. I welcome you to service in the newly awakening and tremendously important continent of Africa.

As a member of the Peace Corps you are offering your skills and knowledge toward the fulfillment of tasks specified by your African hosts. In a very real way you can add to the vitality and stability of the country of your assignment and can contribute to its development in peace and freedom.

You will also learn that Africa has much to teach. You will learn of patience and dignity, of beauty and color. You will be working with people in whom great hopes have been aroused, and you can help them realize some of these hopes.

Beyond this you will be one of the fortunate few Americans abroad who will really engage in "person to person" diplomacy. Yours, therefore, is an enormous responsibility. Your actions and attitudes will greatly influence your new friends and fellow workers in the concepts they hold of America. As our President has said so eloquently . . . "If you can impress /them/ with your commitment to freedom, to the advancement of the interests of people everywhere, to your pride in your country and its best traditions . . . you will make a significant contribution far beyond the immediate day-to-day tasks you may do in the months ahead. . . ."

Service with the Peace Corps is a great opportunity but a demanding one, which requires that you devote a part of your life, with no thought of gain, to your country and to our African friends.

Our best wishes and prayers for success and achievement go with you as you take up this challenge in the service of the Peace Corps and of African-American friendship.

Sincerely yours,

G. Mennen Williams
Assistant Secretary

Letter of January 12, 1962

Dear Folks,

The Ministry called again today for me. As Queens College is a government school (one of the very few in the country), the staff are employees of the Ministry of Education and are expected to stay on the campus during the holidays in the event the Ministry needs them. At the moment they are in a bind trying to tabulate the results of the School Leaving Certificate exams given in December to thousands of students in the Eastern Region. We go down columns of numbers to pick out the passing grades. Today the Ministry decided that 160 at least will be given passing credits. Yesterday it was 170, so we had to go over all the sheets again.

I managed to get to the bank and the post office today, which is an accomplishment as each requires a long wait. Most of the people in line aren't waiting for anything but just talking to someone. They don't move and seem oblivious that it is the bank or post office.

I have a steward named Elias. Elias has helped me scrub and wash and iron these past two days so that I can move into the vacant house. The girl who lives there will return in two weeks so we will be roommates until the end of February, until a house is vacant for me. Elias is going to market for me tomorrow and will start cooking. I think he is going to be very good. I sang him a Yoruba song and asked him if it was alright. He said rather patiently, "Oh Madam is trying!" which was disillusioning until I discovered that he meant by that, that I was terrific!

Today I was carrying a bucket of hardware and it was heavy. All of a sudden I heard a small insistent voice behind me and I stopped, thinking I had dropped something. A little boy was trying to tell me to put it on my head! He was right—that is much the best way to carry things!

Oh, before I forget, my Peace Corps passport is stamped valid only for Nigeria. My other passport is valid until 1963 and I left it at home

... in the top left drawer of my desk. Sometime could you send it to me? My first holiday is not until April. Probably I will not be able to travel until Christmas when I get ten weeks. Non-government schools get their holidays in July and August.

Love,
Dot

Dorothy learns to dance the highlife with a fellow volunteer

Teaching in Nigeria

Thrusting a large, heavy, and worn rifle into my hands, Okafor stood watching me, a broad toothless smile engulfing his face, his eyes sparkling. "Please Madam, you can start the race."

I looked at the students of Queens College, Enugu crouched, with fingertips touching the ground, poised to run. In the stands behind me, students and faculty were all watching me expectantly.

I gulped nervously. I had never touched a gun before. I had been in Nigeria a week, at Queens for three days. Trembling, I turned to Okafor. "I would be so proud if you would start the race," I said, handing him the rifle.

He did.

My ears ringing with the "Boom!" I returned to sit with the faculty.

I was assigned to teach English and history. The two hundred students lived at the school, as in all secondary schools. Frequently students who passed the entrance exams were supported by their entire village, as tuition was high. Secondary schools for girls were rare and Queens was a government school into which it was more difficult to gain entrance. Students felt a lot of pressure to succeed and were unfailingly polite and respectful toward teachers, standing up as they entered or left the classroom.

With my first assignments, I found that students wrote in perfect English with beautiful handwriting, but all of the papers were the same. I asked how this could be so, but was met with silence. I tried creative assignments, such as writing a poem—after carefully explaining what a poem was. There was some variation. One day I assigned a descriptive essay, "I never saw a purple mountain." A minute before the bell rang, a student raised her hand, "Excuse me, Madam, what is purple?" The bell rang. Another hand. "Excuse me, Madam, what is a mountain?" I canceled the assignment.

The curriculum was exactly that of an English school student. No West African curriculum existed yet.

One day as I was attempting to explain Charlemagne, trying to make it relevant, one student raised a hand. "Excuse me, Madam, are you sure this is important?"

The faculty at Queens College quickly welcomed me. One colleague took me to see a leper colony. Another took me to visit an agricultural college. I wrote about these in letters. We had been told that if you ever had a car accident in the bush, you had to keep going. The roads had more people than cars. My colleagues drove fearlessly, careening around women carrying babies on their backs and basins of things to sell at the market on their heads, boys on bicycles, and occasionally lorries stacked with people.

Nigerian women left their parents' homes only when they were married and moved to their husband's compounds. Single white women living alone were a novelty. One day a taxi pulled up to my house and a Nigerian gentleman jumped out. "I've come to marry you!" Politely I refused, hopefully not offending him. He drove off.

I met Aba who was the editor of a newspaper in Enugu and he introduced me to the cultural life of Enugu, the capital of the Eastern Region. I have written in my letters quite a bit about this.

I had a party and invited some Peace Corps volunteers living nearby. One came from Nsukka, Hershel Herzberg. Four months later we were married and I moved to his compound at St. Teresa's College in Nsukka. There is more about this and I describe Hershel to my parents in the letters that follow.

I taught geometry and algebra during July and August. In geometry class, I explained the first theorem and assigned homework. The next day I asked students to explain their work on the board. Because expatriates had names for each day of the week, many students were named Sunday, Monday, Tuesday,… but no Saturday. Students were expected to stand when the teacher entered and left the room, and to sit silently and take notes when the teacher spoke.

I held out a piece of chalk, "Sunday, please do the first problem on the board."

"Oh no, Madam, I cannot!"

"But I know you can."

Shyly, he took the chalk, afraid of offending me. He wrote the problem and turned around to see his classmates' reaction. Silence. Slowly, but with growing confidence, he continued. He completed the problem.

He turned around, barely able to contain his giggle of delight. "That was fun, Madam!"

Thirty hands shot up. "Me, Madam! Me, Madam! Me, Madam!"

"Okay, Thursday, you do problem two. Wednesday, problem three."

A couple of days later in the faculty room one of the Holy Ghost fathers who ran the school demanded, "Mrs. Herzberg what *are* you doing in your classes? My students are raising their hands and asking questions. They say, "but we can in Mrs. Herzberg's class."

Things were never quite the same at St. Teresa's.

Hershel taught history. The students were required to memorize endless details of English history. Sitting in the rain forest in 100-degree heat every day, it seemed incongruous. A West African curriculum would not exist for some years yet.

Living in Nsukka in the bush was very different from Enugu. It rained every day—some 70 inches a year—sometimes light sun showers, sometimes torrential rains with frightful lightning that seemed to hit the ground and light up everything brilliantly. Two students playing on the soccer field in front of our house were struck by lightning and killed while we were there.

Immediately behind our house within a short walk was a village. Walking one day, I came across a group of villagers standing quietly listening to someone. It was in Igbo, so I did not understand. I joined them. After about fifteen minutes they suddenly broke into English. In crisp English accents they said, "Our Father who art in heaven, hallowed be thy name …" The Lord's Prayer in English. Clearly the missionaries had been there.

I began teaching French at the university in September of 1962. It was about a mile from St. Teresa's and the fathers had lent us a car. Building a university in the bush was the creation of Nnamdi

Azikiwe, the first president of an independent Nigeria. Nsukka was his home. He had spent sixteen years in the United States and had enlisted the aid of university officials in the state of Michigan to develop the University of Nigeria, Nsukka, which was modeled on Michigan State University. The faculty came from England, France, Germany, the Philippines, Israel, India, and the United States. Being part of the faculty was delightful. There were already thirty Peace Corps volunteers teaching there.

I describe my classes in my letters though I remember one incident in particular. There was a map of Europe on the wall and one day I went to it and pointed out some of the countries in Europe—France, Italy, Germany, and of course, England. The class erupted in laughter. I was astonished.

"Oh no, Madam, England is *not* so small."

I showed them the names of the countries written on the map. But they would not believe me.

When the class finished in June 1963, some students commented. They wrote: "You are a very good teacher but you have funny maps!"

And now for some of my letters, which expand on my experiences.

Rt. Hon. Dr. Nnamdi Azikiwe, Zik, of Africa, Owelle-Osowa-anya of Onitsha, govenor general of Nigeria from 1960 to 1963, and first president of Nigeria from 1963 to 1966

Queen's College, Enugu

Letter of January 19, 1962

Dear Folks,

Yesterday was quite an experience so I must capture it before it vanishes. I started out for a walk to take some pictures, see the library and the hospital, and just generally find my way around. I stopped in the regional library and was reading a newspaper when someone came up and asked if I was with the Peace Corps and did I remember meeting him last week. I didn't but said I did. He was Aba Abuosa, the regional editor for the *West African Pilot*. We drove downtown and he remembered he had an assignment to finish up. Zik (Nnamdi Azikiwe, governor general of Nigeria) was taking a train from Nsukka to Lagos, stopping at Enugu at noon. Aba was supposed to cover it for his paper. So we went to the station. Zik arrived. He is a buoyant, personable man adored by the whole country, but worshiped by the Igbo, as he is one of them. He was the first Igbo to be educated in the United States—spent fifteen years there and sounds like an American. His return and leadership of the national movement sparked Igbo participation in it. As he approached, the crowd chanted, "Z-I-K." He was surrounded by an entourage but very accessible, walking and shaking hands for several minutes. I took several pictures. Reporters flocked around him with questions.

Afterward we drove to a rest house—which is built like a motel but is the only restaurant in town, and is always full of Europeans and a few Nigerians. Anyone can go there but it is expensive. We collected one of the Peace Corps people teaching in the Government Technical Institute and had lunch. All of a sudden, a man walked in who was an administrator in my UCLA training program. He was with a crowd from Nsukka. He is setting up an adult education program at the University of Nigeria this year. He will be back in April with his family. Anyway, we had a long chat. He will be living at Niger College right across a field from me.

Later Aba picked me up at 6:30 to go to a cocktail party. It was at the Nigerian Broadcasting Company. I met three headmasters of schools around Enugu—all British. One was a delightful Catholic father. The conversation moved around poultry farming and the weather—we still have some harmattan* wind, which leaves things dry and cold. I was given a tour of the broadcasting station—they had installed some new equipment just that morning and it was quite sparkling and impressive. They have a recording room where they record the music of various indigenous talents. They feel they have a responsibility in this as they feel people will simply turn on their radios rather than make their own music, and it will disappear. The radio stations will have the only archives. He mentioned one man who was working with them in Lagos, whose brother lectured to us at UCLA! What a small world!

Love,
Dot

*harmattan—a dry wind that blows from the Sahara

Letter of January 25, 1962
Edward R. Murrow

Dear Folks,

Another week is almost over—it really seems incredible!

Monday Jill Eyoma, my English teacher friend, drove us to Onitsha. We shopped in Onitsha market—supposedly the largest one in West Africa. It is paved, unlike other markets, and the stalls organized and merchandise displayed attractively. I bought material for a tablecloth, a skirt, and a dress. Jill bought some for a dress and a little shirt for her boy. Then we found three PCVs stationed at Onitsha at two different schools. Two were too absorbed with moving in to talk but the third is living with two very nice Irishmen and we had lunch. Onitsha fairly swarms with Irishmen because they find they can make enough money teaching there for one year to make it worthwhile and then go home.

Johnny S is the PCV teaching in Onitsha—you met him I think. He is struggling with sixth form physics, which is college level. This was his first week teaching. He is growing a red beard. He has a very nice house and has bought several pieces of art. We caught up on all the gossip!

Monday night Aba took me to a USIA reception for Edward R. Murrow, the head of the U.S. Information Agency. I met Mr. Murrow and told him I had long admired him. He told me he had just come from Ghana where amidst abrasive discussions of America, he had heard the Peace Corps highly praised. The Ghanians were skeptical at first. That group has been teaching since September. None of the Nigerians or English I talked to really knew who he was. I explained over and over who he was. Americans are just as foreign to the English as to the Nigerians. My headmistress was there and was quite bewildered that I had come with a Nigerian man. She is charming and very proper!

Jill and I have finished our dresses now and even ones for the babies. Wednesday night Aba drove around with two of the PCVs at Nike National Grammar School and I had five guests for dinner. Elias had to go to his village because his father was sick (more likely, however, there was a feast or something). But he brought a friend to help me. So Emmanuel fixed fufu.* This requires several hours, as he had to pound the yams with a pestle until they were like mashed potatoes, but a little tougher. Then he cooks a stew. Everyone takes a handful of yams and dips it into the stew. That is fufu.

The girls begin to return tomorrow and school starts Monday. I will tell you more about my assignments when they become more clear to me!

Love,

Dot

*fufu—Nigerian dish made from yams

Letter of February 12, 1962

Dear Folks,

Thank you very much for all the letters and the tax forms, and the enclosed letter from G. Mennen Williams.* I'm glad the film came back so well. My film finally appeared from England in long negatives with a note saying I would have to pay more for it if I wanted slides or prints. I will send it back again and see what happens.

I am beginning to feel a little more secure in relationships here and in seeing how, or rather what, my role can be. I am constantly visiting, exchanging meals, taking trips with the English teachers at the school (my colleagues) and with members of the English and American community. This is the first time Enugu and vicinity has seen so many Americans. The British are as overwhelmed as the Nigerians!

I was in Afikpo Saturday with the math teacher. She had to meet with the other math teachers in the region to decide on a common entrance examination. Queens is the only girls government school in the region. They fought it out for hours and then we came home. The red dust blown about by the harmattan finally irritated my lungs and finally I caught a cold. Respiratory infections are probably the most common thing next to malaria and dysentery in this country. The heat and dryness make one feel suffocated. And very uncomfortable. Things pass as quickly as they come and today it is all gone.

I had lunch with the wife of the British consul yesterday. She is Swedish and nutty in her own way. He is not an inhibited Britisher at all. Many of the British—at least the ones I meet—say they feel very guilty about Africa and the very different standards of living. But then they say, "After all, what can we do? Their living quarters are frightful but they are used to it." We got into a discussion with the British consul about American Negroes and how Africans identify more with American Negroes than American Negroes identify with them.

One evening at USIS, United States Information Service, a very fine Negro judge from Iowa told the people that there is no desire of American Negroes to come "home" to Africa, they are Americans and love it. They might like to visit Africa sometime but not to stay. Africans approached the Negroes in our group with curiosity. Our colleagues seemed a little embarrassed—they feel as much American here as we do.

They were also concerned about an East German lecturer who has been imported to teach history at the University of Nigeria, Nsukka. He apparently speaks fluent Igbo and has brought an American Negro who has chosen to reside in East Germany as his assistant The American administrators of the university are scheduled to leave in May and of course no one knows what will happen next. From all I hear, the university is doing very well—overcoming its growing pains.

A week ago I went with one of the teachers to a village to see some Juju dancing. Juju refers to any pagan ritual. This was a second burial. We had been invited and had some palm wine with a family beforehand. The dancers were completely concealed with what looked like burlap bags, brightly painted and with colorful yarn attached to a frame, which they carried on their backs. They twisted and turned as they danced. They danced impulsively, each moved as they felt like, jumping at the audience to frighten them. Five boys ran around with huge ancient rifles, which they shot into the air to frighten the evil spirits away. Everyone seemed to enjoy it tremendously. They insisted that we didn't take pictures so we conspicuously put our cameras away. Occasionally I felt the children touching or pulling my arm to touch an Onytsha (white woman). It was a wonderful experience. I love the villages—there is an irresistible vitality, which emanates from the people—unspoiled, imaginative, and alive!!

Love,
Dot

*G. Mennen Williams was the assistant secretary of state under President John F. Kennedy.

Letter of February 17, 1962

Dear Folks,

It's a lazy Sunday morning and I have nothing to do but correct eighty notebooks and plan next week's classes. But I have to tell you about yesterday before I forget anything!

An English lecturer and I went to a jubilee celebration at the Oji River leper colony—commemorating their twenty-fifth year. We went around the wards, which were all spruced up for the occasion and saw demonstrations teaching what leprosy is and how it is cured. It can now be completely cured by tablets in two years if caught in time. It is a disease of the nerves and skin. The deformities associated with it are the result of carelessness, as the leper cannot feel pain and burns himself, causing ulcers. They are trying to teach the patients to take care of themselves so that when they operate and replace nerves, muscles, and skin, they will have a normal body. The work they are doing in orthopedic surgery, physical therapy, and rehabilitation is breathtaking. Some patients even still are rejected by their families and their villages who don't want to know where they are. But the fear of the disease has largely disappeared. The people are also learning to report themselves or others when they suspect the disease—rather than hiding it, although many still hide it.

Hundreds came yesterday, wandering around with the patients, which wouldn't have been possible ten years ago.

During the 1950s, twenty-five thousand patients were released. Last year a former leper married a non-leper, which was a sensation the whole community hasn't forgotten. The number in the settlement has been reduced to about two hundred. The number of children affected has been cut in half, although there is a small school in the settlement with patients as teachers. There are Boy Scout and Girl Guides groups, choirs, dance groups, etc. There are handicraft shops, which make beautiful things. We watched dancing in the afternoon—some Igbo groups imported and one group of patients. They were excellent and impressive evidence of inexhaustible creative energy. One man stood some 25–30 feet above the group on stilts and bounced and jumped and whirled remarkably.

After supper we went to a pageant portraying the twenty-five years of the settlement. From buying the lad from a chief to the arrival of the first patients. It included graphic scenes of the painful injection of thick oil, to the arrival of new drugs, and finally the discharge of thousands. They also acted out the precautions a leper must take not to injure himself and showed the corrections possible with surgery. Nearly all the patients acted in the pageant and most of the staff as well!

Love,
Dot

Letter of February 24, 1962

… Next week I move into my own house. I sacked my steward or rather he sacked himself by getting into trouble and being put in jail. I have a new steward named Isiah. He is an Efik boy. He is very bright and has never been a cook steward before. It's Sunday morning and he is learning to fix one piece of bacon, one egg, and one piece of toast for me under the guidance of Ms. Heanshaw's steward. He is a delight!

Letter of March 4, 1962

Dear Folks,

About the teaching, well let's see. I teach one class of third form English to fifteen-year-olds. This consists of poetry—lyrics and ballads, such as the "Rime of the Ancient Mariner." Then *The Merchant of Venice*—the first time they have had Shakespeare—and Jane Eyre. I've never taught Shakespeare before and it is quite an experience. I started by having them write an essay on Elizabethan drama and draw a picture of the theater. Then I talked about anti-Semitism in England in the 1600s and the theme of the "pound of flesh" and the "three caskets." They take parts reading it and do very well. Once they understand the vocabulary, it amazes me how well they understand it. I try desperately to explain the humor and can only hope they catch it. So much they must grasp only intellectually—it is so removed from their experience.

Then I have a history class of second form—only their second year in high school. Most have had some five to six years of primary school previously. They are a joy—eager to learn and insatiably curious about things. We were reviewing the Roman Empire, which they had last year, and winding through the rise of Christianity.

Then I am form mistress for one of our two streams of first form. My form is doing very well. I have them for English and history. They take geography, history, English, arithmetic, math, science, biology, needlework, physical education, and singing. I take all of the first form for singing where I am trying to teach them to read music. I have already taught them ten spirituals. I am taking just my little first form to visit the House of Assembly in Enugu this week.

Love,
Dot

Letter of March 20, 1962

Dear Folks,

I thought when I moved into my house life would settle down, but no such luck. Everyone expects me to throw a little party to warm it. So I am doing it! It is Saturday. Before then I have to finish the pillows for my chairs. Then the Eastern House of Assembly is meeting in Enugu. I went to a session yesterday afternoon and tonight there is a cocktail party. Then some Australian friends who are moving to Lagos have asked me to dinner tonight … and so it goes!

The last two weekends have been wonderful. One I spent in Ogute, the village of one of the Nigerian teachers on the staff. She is quite wealthy. Her papa is such fun. We christened a gorgeous Rolls-Royce they have just bought "Alexander the Great" with some champagne. Nigerians spend their money on cars, big houses but the furnishings and the clothes they wear don't change as radically. It seems to me they have little interest in investing in art, books, etc. as yet.

Then last weekend I went with one of the English teachers to meet with a missionary couple at Asaba Rural Training College just across the Niger from Onitsha. It is quite a trip because one has to take a ferry across the Niger, which may or may not come, and one may or may not get on when it does. One has to back down a steep ramp and maneuver on two pieces of metal to get on. Then your car provides the seating accommodations for the pedestrians. Finally you arrive behind a big lorry with people clinging to all sides of it. The Rural Training College at Asaba is really something to see—poultry farms, livestock breeding, experimental gardens, fishponds, veterinary hospital, two hundred students, seventy-five teachers in training and thirty-five girl students doing domestic science, I guess.

The American missionary couple we were visiting were quite interesting. They spent twenty-five years in India. She is an ear, nose, and throat doctor. They raised four children and all of them are doctors now!! They drew comparisons with Nigeria. One was the attitude toward manual labor. It is just despised in Nigeria, for example, when the boys from Asaba go back to their villages. They are just laughed at for going to school and coming back a farmer! It is one occupation everyone is escaping from. Compared to India, Nigerians are much healthier on the whole. They also saw in Nigeria trees dripping with mangoes, bananas—fruit of every kind. In India these would be stripped bare. They find the Nigerian villagers far harder to communicate with than the villagers in India—but they didn't know why. They find Nigerians generally more garrulous and aggressive.

I've seen two plays now done by Nigerian drama groups. One was a local group that needed more practice. The other, a group from the University of Ibadan. They were superb! Nigerians are natural extroverts and with a little inspiration do very fine acting! They did a Nigerian version of *The Taming of the Shrew* with comedy bits in pidgin English and doing the highlife. Very well done! Their sense of timing was excellent and delightful!

Love,
Dot

Letter of March 28, 1962

Dear Folks,

I love my little house—my housewarming was very nice. Now that the House of Assembly is in session, Enugu is flooded with all kinds of interesting faces. One of the members of Parliament and I went up to Nsukka to see the University of Nigeria yesterday—there was a public holiday for Youth Day. All over Nigeria youth march in their school uniforms and in the afternoon participate in athletic competitions. Nsukka is surviving somehow—the most recent occurrence is a bitter split in the student body on procedural matters concerning student government. There is some suspicion that one of the student leaders has absconded with quite a bit of money and the chancellor has closed the Student Union until an investigation has been made. One faction has criticized him for this—exactly what happened is not clear. Otherwise Nsukka is doing fine.

I don't know if I told you some of the jokes which are emerging. So I will include them here:

One of the agriculturalists at Asaba told this. In a chicken yard where one proud rooster reigned, the rooster was making his daily rounds when he noticed some turkeys in the next yard. He approached closer and noticed particularly their eggs, remarking on their size. He called all of his hens together and pointed this out saying, "I want you to notice what they are doing in the next community."

One of the PCV teachers near here was giving his first lectures on physics, developing the concept of mass. He described its properties of weight, quantity, etc.—basic concepts of physics. Finally, folding up his notes he turned to the class and said, "Can anyone tell me what is mass?" One student said immediately, "Yes sir. Mass is a religious service of the Catholic Church!" to which the teacher calmly replied, "Tomorrow we will have the last sacraments," and walked out (it is a Catholic school).

Love,
Dot

Letter of April 10, 1962

Dear Folks,

There have been a lot of activities at the school.

First, we had Youth Day in which the whole school marched at the stadium together with all the other schools in the Enugu area. The finals for all of Nigeria of the Women's Athletic Association events were held in the sports stadium. All those who had won in their region competed—the North, West, East, and Lagos. It was really very exciting! The West won the first two races and the East won everything else. It's always this way apparently because the Igbos, at the moment, are the best athletes. There were very few from the North, but people are beginning to feel that when or if the North does catch up, both in opportunities and educational facilities where athletics can be organized, they will offer the real competition. They were not very good at all this year. The resources of the North have hardly been touched.

Last week things were disrupted while we got ready for Open Day when the community visits Queens. They came at 4:00 p.m. and listened to a speech by Mrs. Kirkpatrick and then one by the minister of education. Then prizes were awarded to the leading girl in each subject and the leading girl in each class. Some of them came as a surprise to me I must say! Now I have some clue as to who should be working harder!

Then beginning Monday, April 9, the Festival of Arts for the Eastern Region descended. Monday morning I went to Women's Training College just across the field here, to judge English storytelling. Then all Monday afternoon all of the secondary schools presented one act plays. Queens School was by far the best in acting, timing, presentation, etc. But the judges decided that historical plays were not appropriate for a Nigerian festival of the arts and our play was about the Siege of Calais by the English. So we got second.

Then yesterday the schools presented the same speech from Julius Caesar where the senators stab him. Very exciting! Most of the schools didn't show up but of the five who entered, Queens came first. This was largely due to our crowd scene and to our Brutus. Brutus was played by the most brilliant girl in the school—Pat Otue. She just got distinctions in every subject she took for her certificate. She spent five years in Canada and one year in New York (Buffalo) while her father was studying to be a doctor. She has just taken a scholarship exam to go to America. I can't imagine a better student. She had to go to an interview before a formidable panel who asked her her feelings about discrimination. Maybe she will be at a university in America by September!

Today there were the musicals—so through our classes bagpipes floated, played by Nigerians, then flute solos, and finally pianos. Each instrument is given a set piece to play.

There is a meeting of all UCLA PCVs at Kaduna in a few weeks to evaluate our program. Not all of us will be able to be there. They are keen on evaluations because there is a rumor that there are three hundred more PCVs coming! I hope they don't move them in on us!

Love,
Dot

Letter of May 2, 1962

Dear Folks,

I realize it has been some time since I have written and now I don't know where to begin.

Somewhere out of time and space I have met someone special and we are going to be married at the end of this month in Lagos! His name is Hershel Herzberg and he is a PCV teaching at St. Teresa's College in Nsukka. He teaches upper forms history and English. He has done some graduate work in history. His mother lives now in New York but he has spent most of his life in San Francisco.

Hersh has to work on the Nigerian census—which means trailing out into the bush to count the people—until the middle of May. Then we hope to arrange a Jewish wedding in Lagos. There are so many obstacles at the moment—we both only have the last two weeks of

May for a vacation. We don't know whether we will be stationed together immediately—we are both very happy where we are at the moment. The Peace Corps office is very reluctant to put someone else at Nsukka—there are already thirty PCVs at the university. The Peace Corps office knows about us and is working on things. Really we can do very little until we get to Lagos.

School has ended for this term at Queens. We had staff meetings for the last two days and discussed every girl in the school. Each teacher contributes her comments in writing and then a general statement emerges for each girl. Most interesting to do. Surprising how many different impressions there were of a student—for one teacher she was excellent, for another very poor. Then we had more sports competition between houses within Queens. All of them won something except one house, which apparently loses every year! Sports events must be run this term because now the rainy season begins in earnest and unpredictable moments make it impossible to schedule events.

We are going up to Nsukka now. While he is doing the census I have some hundreds of exams to correct. We invigilated (supervised) the Queens School entrance exams about three weeks ago—they were given at centers all over the Eastern Region and the Queens school staff had to invigilate them. I went to Onitsha with Hersh. Some three thousand little girls take them each year. This year sixty will be selected—it has been only thirty in previous years. The school is growing. Anyway, the exams consist of English and math. I am correcting the math. Last year it was too hard and eliminated too many. So far I haven't found anyone who has more than eight points out of fifty.

We will write soon and send some pictures.

Love,

Dot and Hersh

38 Me, Madam

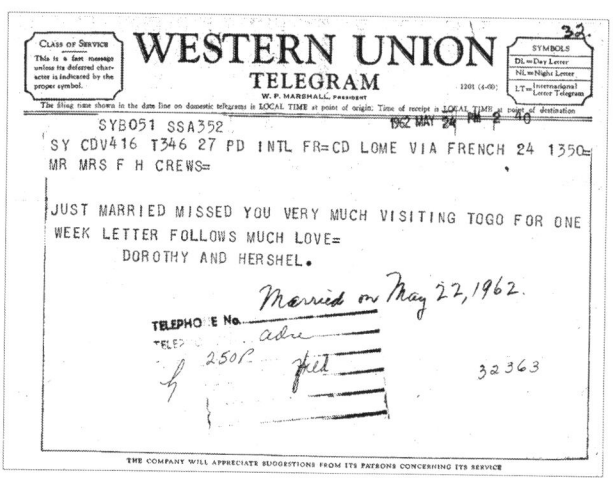

```
WESTERN UNION
TELEGRAM

SYB051 SSA352                         1962 MAY 24
SY CDV416 T346 27 PD INTL FR=CD LOME VIA FRENCH 24 1350=
MR MRS F H CREWS=

JUST MARRIED MISSED YOU VERY MUCH VISITING TOGO FOR ONE
WEEK LETTER FOLLOWS MUCH LOVE=
    DOROTHY AND HERSHEL.
```
Married on May 22, 1962.

The Census

Hershel signed on as enumerator for the census, and went with other enumerators into the villages. The way that he tried to count how many people lived in each compound was to approach one of the houses. The children would run up to greet him. He would ask who lived in that house.

The children would all shout, "We do."

He carefully wrote down their names and ages, and the names and ages of the adults.

Then he would go to another house in the compound. The same children would run after him, delighted with this new game. He would again ask who lived in the house. Again they all shouted, "We do."

That happened at every house in the compound.

When the statistics were assembled, it was found the number of women counted could not possibly have had the number of children counted.

Enumerators did discover a village of three thousand people deep in the bush that no one had known of before, but ultimately the census was discarded.

Letter of May 14, 1962

Dear Folks,

Today is Census Day!

Hersh has been doing the preliminary work of testing local chiefs, counselors, and anyone else who wants to try to select enumerators. Some of the material he uses I have gathered copies of and will send you. Last night at midnight was the census moment when bells were to be rung in every compound to remind people to count and remember who was sleeping in their compound that night. That's where they would be counted.

Trying to organize the enumeration districts on the basis of the 1952 census hasn't been too accurate, as the population has grown enormously. The section around Nsukka is one of the most heavily populated in Nigeria. I've been going around with him. On market days thousands emerge from the bush. Most have never seen a white woman, and the only white men are the Catholic fathers. So every white man is "father." Whenever we stop they press around the car to see me. At one village, Enugu-Isike, I got out and played with the children for hours.

I am still correcting exams. I have done about five hundred now and hope to do another two hundred more before we leave. We hope to leave tomorrow morning. We discovered from talking to some Israeli people that there is no rabbi in Nigeria, so we are trying to get in touch with the Israeli ambassador who can perform the ceremony, or a captain of a ship from Israel that happens to be in the harbor. The Peace Corps has agreed that I will be in Nsukka, so that much is settled. Father Butler, the headmaster of Hersh's school, has given us the car for the trip, which is very lucky. The staff here is very lively and very nice. St. Teresa's has three hundred boys from Forms 1–5. The students are good but not of the capability of Queen's School students. But I shan't lose touch with Queens—I have lots of friends there.

First row center, left to right: Dorothy, Father Butler, and Hershel

Anyway, we hope to be in Lagos and married, and back here the end of next week to begin the term. We just might go to Dahomey for our honeymoon—it is only a day from Lagos to a charming little town we have heard of.

Thank you so much the copies of the *New York Times Book Review*. We both pour over them avidly and are so thirsty to see some of the books described. The Peace Corps has been sending the "Sunday News of the Week" in *Review of the Times*. We also get *Time*, *Life*, and *New Republic*. Never have I read *Time* and *Life* so avidly. But I must say I can't stand *New Republic*. I leave my magazines in the Queens library when I finish with them—some of the staff read them.

Are those books really coming? I would prefer they were sent to Queens since that is where they are expected.

Must stop now. I've been following the story of the trees in the backyard from chapter to chapter. Don't let the little cherry tree go please!

The weather is delightful. It is the rainy season. Every time it gets a little humid, it rains and everything is cool and beautiful again. This is the most delightful part of the year and will last till the end of August. By then we hope to have a garden …

Love,
Dot

Letter of May 31, 1962

Dear Folks,

We just returned from our honeymoon yesterday and I opened the letters from you—none had arrived as yet when we left. I will tell you about the ceremonies and honeymoon but first about Hershel.

He is 6 foot 2, black hair, brown eyes, and a mustache. He is sensitive, intelligent, occasionally shy, loves steaks and salads and good food. He finished his BA at University of California, Berkeley in political science. He knows all the professors I knew there. He went to law school for a while, then two years in the army, which he spent in Germany. So he speaks German. Then he went back to school, still not sure of what he wanted to do so he got a teaching credential; then began with the Peace Corps last July. He was with a group that trained for six months before he started teaching—not entirely intentional but as the first PCVs, no one knew quite what to do with them. He was at Harvard for three months, then at University College, Ibadan for three months. He knew Marjorie Michelmore and of course all that group was caught up in that incident. Although his group finished practice teaching sometime in November I believe, they did not go out to begin teaching until we arrived on December 28.

He teaches most of the history at St. Teresa's College. Now he feels that he wants to go back to law school. He has a brother who is a professor of bacteriology at University of Florida, Gainesville. This summer he is teaching at University of California, Berkeley. Hershel thinks he wants to return there. His name is Dr. Mendel Herzberg. He has another brother, David. Both David and Mendel are in their forties. His father died when he was young and he doesn't remember him. His mother remarried and now lives in New York City.

Now about the wedding. We left Enugu on Tuesday, May 15 and arrived in Lagos on Thursday—spending one night in Benin and one in Ibadan. In Lagos I stayed with Jake and Fran Todd, two of the Peace Corps (PC) administration. Hersh stayed at the parliamentary flats. This is the very same place I first stayed when we arrived in December. Two PCVs stationed in Lagos live there permanently and found him a room.

We wanted to go to Dahomey for our honeymoon so had to get visas and international driver's licenses. The fathers of St. Teresa's insisted that we take the car. We completed the forms for our marriage license. We talked to the Israeli ambassador and discovered that only a rabbi can perform an official Jewish wedding. So, in order to be legally married we would have to have a civil ceremony. So we went back to the Marriage Bureau on Monday and did this. A little man wandered in with a camera so there are a few pictures of this but not very good. Two of our PCV friends came along as witnesses and they look rather startled. I bought material on Saturday for a dress, gloves, shoes, veil, etc. The four families connected with the PC administration in Lagos helped me shop. They know a dressmaker. She measured me and the dress was ready Monday. We arrived at the ceremony at the Israeli Embassy at 5:30 on Tuesday, May 22. Hersh spent the morning scrambling for papers for Dahomey while the PC doctor's wife fixed my hair.

After the ceremony the Ashabrenners (part of the PC administration) gave us a reception entirely unexpected, with an enormous cake and presents! Everyone was so generous—it was incredible. Then the man who had done the service, Mr. S and his wife, invited us to dinner. They turned out to be a Hungarian Jewish couple. He had a fantastic collection of African masks with which he expects to open a museum in Israel when they go back. We spent the night in Lagos and then drove on to Togo the next morning.

It is only a two-hour drive from Lagos to the Dahomey border. From there it is an hour to Cotonou, a beautiful obviously French town on the ocean. We had lunch and drove another two hours to Togo, now a French territory under UN auspices. We stayed at Le Benin, an enormous modern hotel in Lomé right on the ocean with also a swimming pool. The ocean drops off quickly there so there were ships anchored only about one thousand yards offshore. It was a beautiful spot but expensive so we could only stay two days.

One day while looking for a place to buy film we met a little Lebanese businessman named Guillaume (William) who insisted that he had nothing better to do but to show us where to go. After we found a place to buy film and paints and canvases, he took us out for drinks and an incredibly delicious lunch of lobster. We never did find out much about Guillaume but we'll never forget that lobster!

We drove back to Lagos and spent one night, then drove on to Ibadan. I had an attack of gastritis and we had to stay two days there, which was really nice as Hersh knew Ibadan and wanted to visit places. There were lots of PCVs vacationing in Ibadan so we saw lots of friends. Just Friday the day before we arrived, there had been riots in the Western House of Assembly and there was talk of the federal government taking over the region under martial law until elections could be held. However, now it is a week later and there is still talk—the riots went no further than within the House itself. The Action Group—the opposition party—in the West has broken down and the government is momentarily immobilized.

We left Ibadan and spent that night, the 29th in Benin. We stopped for lunch with a PCV at Ife, and in Benin City visited PCVs with the first Peace Corps baby. She is three weeks old! An AID (Agency for International Development) staff person in town likes to put up PCVs. So we had a marvelous place to stay. He is beginning a rubber plantation here. He has been in Ceylon for years. He got up to chat and have breakfast with us at 6:00 a.m.

We drove straight on to Enugu although crossing the Nige River at Asaba took almost three hours. It always seems miraculous every time one completes a trip in the Asaba ferry to Onitsha. It is indescribable but sometime I will try to capture it. We packed my things in Enugu and came to Nsukka.

For the next two months or so I will teach maths, and maybe a little English at St. Teresa's. Then I will teach French at the University at Nsukka.

Love,
Dot

Students at Queen's School

St. Teresa's College, Nsukka

Nsukka is deep in the bush. Traveling north fifty miles from Enugu is an experience—red dirt roads wide enough for one car, barefoot women carrying heavy loads on their heads and babies tied to their backs, joined by bicyclists all going in the same direction to the nearest market. Finally a one-room building marked "Post Office" would appear. Then you would see a gas station and a dry goods store, and you would have arrived. Nsukka!

We picked up our mail every week at the post office which was surprisingly efficient. Rolls of film sent to England to be developed arrived within a couple of weeks. Packages of shoes and clothes sent from America always made it. And over a hundred letters written home made it as well. At the gas station, it was wise to put your gas in your own car, as the attendant might add a little water. And the store fortunately never ran out of tuna fish and peanut butter, which were important sources of protein. Big animals such as cattle and horses could not survive in the bush because of the tsetse fly, which caused sleeping sickness in animals, but not humans. Chickens, another source of protein, ran wild in the village which meant they had very little meat on them. Eggs were scarce. Nigerians believed that if a woman ate eggs, especially a pregnant woman, she was eating another person's baby. So women were deprived of a valuable source of protein.

Students at St. Teresa's College

Our steward, Isaiah, enjoying the kittens

Settling In

Besides receiving instruction from three Holy Ghost fathers from Ireland, the two hundred boys of St. Teresa's were taught by three Irish couples, a teacher from India, Vanchee, a Nigerian man who had a wife and three children, Hershel, and me. Classes ended each day around 1:00 p.m. and everyone returned to their houses to eat lunch and perhaps take a little siesta. Markets closed, stores closed, and people stayed indoors during the hottest time of the day. About 4:00 p.m. everything opened again.

Between our house and the classrooms was a soccer field. The boys played soccer every day from 4:00 p.m. until dark. We were told a story of a Baptist missionary who felt the boys should have shoes. He ordered sneakers sent from America. The boys put them on. But when they ran they stumbled and fell. They missed the ball and fell into each other. After about an hour, they took off the sneakers and continued barefoot.

Twice during our stay boys were struck by lightning on the soccer field and died. It rained every day. The rain forest got about 70 inches a year. Sometimes it was gentle sun showers that one learned to ignore. Anything that got wet was dry within half an hour. Sometimes it was torrential rains with giant jagged flashes of lightning that lit up the field like daylight. The thunder was angry and loud.

We were awakened each morning by children running through the bush to a nearby primary school. They were required to wear clothes in school. To keep their clothes dry they kept them in boxes on their heads. Arriving at school, they stopped and put the clothes on. When school was over they took them off and ran home. Their heads bobbing up and down, they shouted and laughed as they ran.

I brought my steward, Isaiah, from Enugu, and my two kittens. Isaiah would go to the market and shop and prepare our lunch every day. I knew the villagers ate dogs and cats. But Isaiah adored them and took loving care of the three or four litters they produced.

My adventures teaching algebra and geometry during July and August 1962, I will leave for my letters to tell. The students were unfailingly polite and respectful. They were a joy to teach.

Letter from Hershel of June 8, 1962

Dear Mr. and Mrs. Crews,

    Dottie and I are finally getting settled after our return from Lagos. We had good driving conditions on our return from Lomé, so we were fairly lucky. About the only difficulty we had was an attack of gastritis that bothered Dottie in Ibadan. It lasted only a day, however, and Murray Frank, the Western Region Peace Corps Representative at whose home we were staying, obtained a doctor. When Dottie felt better, we stayed in Ibadan an extra day so she could rest before the long journey to Benin and then across the Niger to Enugu. Since I had spent three months training in Ibadan and knew the city and university rather well, we spent a pleasant day sightseeing.

    Once in Enugu, it only took us two trips to bring most of Dottie's things to Nsukka in our car. A truck from the University of Nigeria (at Nsukka) was in Enugu on an errand and Jack Wilmore got it to carry Dottie's trunk and some other bulky things to Nsukka.

    Dottie and I are teaching twenty-four class periods each. We just obtained an Igbo tutor yesterday and we will begin lessons thrice weekly next week. What with extracurricular activities—I'm coaching soccer and basketball this season and administering the school library; Dottie is the leader of St. Teresa's marching fife and drum corps and will soon be teaching dancing at the Queen of the Rosary girls school down the road—we should be kept busy this term.

    I hope that you will have an opportunity to meet my parents soon and show them the wedding pictures. We will try to send some pictures of St. Teresa's soon.

Dottie has told me much about you and I look forward to meeting you.
Warmest Regards, *Hershel*

Letter of June 10, 1962

Dear Folks,

I am very excited about the books. I was in the university library yesterday and it desperately needs books. The law library section consists of one shelf. The French section is two shelves. I see that it will not be possible for me to borrow a French dictionary, which I desperately need for the class in the fall. If you can find *Cassell's New French Dictionary* around the house, probably in my room shelves, please could you send it as fast as possible? Also a French grammar book. I don't know what I have there. I have been reading through some of the French books I brought and enjoy them more than ever.

St Teresa's is sparking up. The staff has begun several projects—a newspaper, magazine, and several science and history societies. And last night I began a chorus. All of the third, fourth, and fifth forms were invited which made over a hundred boys. Some of them are quite enormous! I taught them some spirituals. Their musical vocabulary consists of Catholic masses, highlife, and rock 'n' roll. They caught on immediately and their voices are overwhelming. They are much easier to work with than girls! They will accept a sensible answer to a question, girls will quibble over it! They loved the rhythm, simplicity, and basic emotion of the spirituals. A little Irish girl with a beautiful voice is helping me. But Irish ballads with their dialogue and more subtle rhythms are far too complicated for the boys at this moment. I think they might like Stephen Foster songs and I am practicing again on the guitar as I think they might like American folk music. They are really thirsty for it and it seems like most of the staff might come too. There is such a dearth of cultural life at Nsukka. In a way it is a more "Peace Corps" setting than Enugu. The university being here is changing this, but only beginning.

We just got your letters about talking to Mrs. Mark (Hershel's mother). I am so glad you have finally met.

Every once in a while we get surprising visits from PCVs traveling through on their vacations. Two of them came yesterday for chop (dinner). They were from Kaduna. It was wonderful to show them around Nsukka and they were incredulous at the university. They are comparing schools. The College of Kaduna where they are is not nearly as well equipped as the schools they have seen.

Love,
Dot

Letter of June 11, 1962

Dear Folks,

Wow, housekeeping is a chore anywhere I suppose—but in Africa it is truly exhausting. We tried to work out a schedule for the steward last week—Christopher—who had been Hersh's steward since January so that taking care of two instead of one would not be too much, but he grew more and more sullen and finally refused to do anything. So Hersh had to fire him. Until he left at the end of the month we had to keep everything locked up.

After one has finished marketing and then washing and putting away the food, then boiled water to put in the filter, then boiled water to wash clothes with, then boiled water to cook the vegetables, then ground the meat because it is too tough to eat otherwise, and then dusted everything, you are almost finished. You are ready to iron only to discover that when you took the iron to be fixed, they removed the regulator so everything you touch turns to lace. Then the filter doesn't work and must be cleaned, then the drain is stopped up, then everything you put out to dry fell down in the rainstorm, and the kittens who had to stay in the house made messes everywhere. Meanwhile, people are running in and out together with a dog and another cat. The community on St. Teresa's compound is very close.

Finally, however, we bought new pillows for our five living room chairs and material for drapes which we made. The kitchen is

St. Teresa's College 51

THE WHITE HOUSE
WASHINGTON

June 25, 1962

Dear Mr. Herzberg:

You will soon complete your first year of service in the Peace Corps.

At home and abroad, the Peace Corps has been recognized as a genuine and effective expression of the highest ideals and the best traditions of our Nation. You and your fellow Volunteers have made that judgment possible.

I am proud of your participation, and I trust that in your second year of service your conduct and performance will continue to reflect credit upon you and the Peace Corps.

Sincerely,

John F. Kennedy

Hershel in his second year of service

emerging more efficient bit by bit. We bought a shortwave radio and can now hear the BBC, Ghana, Leopoldville, Brazzaville, Germany, Italy, French Africa, and other places we haven't discovered yet.

I will get my own desk this week so the stacks of papers will dissolve. I made some cookies which came out alright and now I will attempt a pie. We had invited all the Catholic fathers we know around here for dinner this week and some of the PCVs we know from the university. There was a dance last Saturday night. I loved it! I have learned to twist since coming to Nigeria. It is really a legitimate dance!

Did you get a copy of *The Volunteer* in which they printed a long excerpt from a contribution I made to the *Nigeria Volunteer* newsletter? I will send you a copy if I can find it.

It's fun being married! We hope to get a steward next week. I think I will enjoy the Nsukka community when I have a chance to get to know them!

Love,
Dot

Letter of June 16, 1962

Dear Folks,

We have not yet found a steward and the housework is getting us both down. The red dust blows in every day. Just when a meal is almost ready the cooking gas finishes. We have a washerman but with the showers and changes in the weather, there seems to be a constant pile of things to be washed.

Yesterday the Indian education officer who lives next door to us—a marvelous little man from South India named Raj Vancheewaren—helped me figure out how to unplug the drain. After pouring nitric acid down, it didn't work. We brought two men working on a nearby building over and dug a hole to find the pipe. After poking and pushing, huge gobs of stuff came rushing out. It must have been clogged up for months. Now we have padded the hole with large rocks, and left the pipe uncovered so it won't happen again.

I've been doing a lot of cooking—at least I've discovered how to transform the few ingredients available into several different meals. I thought you might like to have some idea of what we eat approximately.

Breakfast: Eggs, dry cereal (corn flakes, rice krispies), toast, coffee. Hersh likes tuna fish, anchovies, blue cheese on bread or crackers.

Lunch: Vegetables, such as spinach known as green-green is very cheap, eggplant (known as garden eggs) fried in groundnut oil, green beans, fresh corn, cabbage. Starch: plantain (kind of a banana which you fry), rice or macaroni, yams—like enormous potatoes. Have a bland taste. The staple food for most of Nigerians. Can flavor with chili sauce or chutney. Can be mashed or boiled. Meat: chicken or beef. Market day is every other day when they kill the cows, if there are any. The meat is fresh but tough. We bought a grinder and can now have hamburgers and meat loaf. Meat will spoil quickly so we often resort to tuna fish. We take vitamins!

Dinner: Same as lunch. I might add fruit salad. Fruit is plentiful and delicious. Pineapple, bananas, pawpaw (a kind of melon), mangoes, oranges, huge grapefruit. Sweets (as the English say for dessert): baking things like banana cake, raspberry pie, and oatmeal cookies.

Before I forget, Hersh loves salads: avocados with onions, cucumbers with onions, parsley with onions.

Tonight two of the Holy Ghost fathers who have spent most of their lives living in the bush around here are coming to dinner. The dinner I plan is: soup (packaged or canned), tuna Fish whirl—tuna fish in dough with mushroom sauce, green beans, fresh corn, banana cake with pineapple, coffee.

St. Teresa's has just given entrance exams. I have 230 of the math parts to correct. This weekend. I collected all of my students' notebooks, which means I have 120 of those to correct also.

One of the PCVs in the Nsukka group is making pizza tomorrow night for dinner. We had dinner with them last night. We have a standing invitation every Thursday if we want. Sometimes the same PCV makes an exquisite spaghetti sauce. He is Italian.

I almost got a desk this week but it wouldn't fit in the door. It is sitting on the porch. The school carpenters will make another one with specifications so it will fit.

A little man just came by trying to sell me seeds. We still hope to have a vegetable garden.

Oh, you keep asking about the money: 1 shilling = about 15 cents; 1 pound = about $2.80; 1 guinea + 1 pound = 1 shilling.

We spend 8-9 pounds per week which is allowing for entertaining. A small boy for help earns about 5 pounds a month. An experienced steward can earn 7-8 pounds a month.

Love,
Dot

Letter of June 24, 1962

Dear Folks,

Father Butler, the principal, moved in a desk for me, which is marvelous. We had an ironing board made by the school carpenter, which is just perfect. We spent Sunday afternoon with machete and hoe chopping the bush behind our house to make a vegetable garden. We can buy many vegetables in the market—which is not nearly as large as Enugu,—but we hope to grow turnips, parsley, beets, melon, beans, and some others which we can't buy. We brought my little boy Isaiah up from Enugu and he is doing very well. It is a hard job for him doing the washing and cleaning for two people. I am teaching him some baking and am also going to begin math lessons in the afternoons so that maybe he can pass the entrance exam and go on to secondary school. He is very bright and willing to learn.

I'm sure I mentioned the kittens before. They provide endless amusement and are about five months old now. Isaiah adores them. Since villagers eat cats and dogs, he has never played with kittens before. They are always getting locked in a closet or closed in a desk drawer, or caught in the wire protecting the windows.

Last Saturday I bought ten ledgers, which we have transformed into weekly school diaries. I also bought eighteen cups and saucers and spoons so we can have staff tea each morning.

Last week one of my students died one morning. So classes were canceled and the staff and most of the boys went to the funeral. It was held in a primary school in a village near St. Teresa's. The school was a rectangular stone building with no partitions, also used as a church. There must have been fifty people, mostly tiny children, chanting Latin prayers and Igbo songs. Funerals occur almost every day. Then, in the pouring rain everyone moved outside where he was buried. Usually someone is buried in their own compound. His parents were not there as they are not Christian. His older brother was his guardian and had the authority to say what kind of ceremony he would have. Although he was my student, he didn't submit any work the first week and some very poor work, so I didn't have a chance to know him.

Today as we were sitting in class we heard drums. There were some three hundred people on one of St. Teresa's fields celebrating the Blessed Sacraments of Corpus Christie. They chanted endlessly all morning moving in a procession from St. Teresa's to another school. The school band was playing in full uniform. Students from St. Teresa's and Queen of the Rosary were in school uniforms. Some little first formers were dressed in white robes and red shirts as altar boys. One of the fathers was carrying the Sacrament fastened to a gold rod. Four little boys carried a canopy over him. Some old pagan chiefs of the area joined the procession with crosses around their necks.

It fascinates the villagers to watch "Europeans" go through such pageantry with such seriousness. It seems an easy leap to go from Juju superstitions to the Catholic pageantry—both mysterious. Afterward, they returned to their villages to participate in Juju rituals. Essentially many, if not most, of the villagers remain pagan. We heard of many instances of Africans returning from Europe, Australia, etc. with college degrees, speaking several languages, slowly become reabsorbed. They begin wearing African dress, participating in rituals like returning to a former self!

I got a letter from Mrs. Sealy and told Queens School about the books. I don't know if their library can hold a thousand books, but somehow they will be distributed around the school. Some will be brought to St. Teresa's.

We talked to the head of the arts faculty and he would be delighted to have me teach French. There are five hundred students who signed up and only two teachers, both of whom are leaving! The University of Nigeria, Nsukka is attempting to cater to thousands of students who cannot afford to go to Ibadan or Ife. Two universities alone cannot accommodate everyone. So the students have finished fifth or sixth form and been out working for years. They are older, anxious to learn, and hard workers. The faculty is good but transient—many coming from Michigan State sources. There are thirty PCVs teaching at the university already.

Love,
Dot

Father Butler, principal of St. Teresa's College

Letter of July 5, 1962

Dear Folks,

Your letters have been wonderful and I will keep you informed immediately on the books. Mrs. Kirkpatrick, the headmistress of Queen's College, has the copy of the letter "Operation Bookshelf" sent to me at Queens College. I also wrote the Peace Corps office in Lagos that the books are coming. They are not marked "Peace Corps" and I did not know if any duty would be charged.

Sitting around the staff room—which has become a hub of activity since I began tea during morning break—we suddenly realized there were Nigerian, Irish, Indian, and Americans present—all formerly English colonies! We were talking about Algerians fighting for independence from the French ...

Letter of July 10, 1962

Dear Folks,

I have a cold and Hersh has a sore neck or something, and we are both exhausted. The whole school went to Onitsha Sunday to watch St. Teresa's play soccer with Christ the King College, another school run by the Holy Ghost fathers, and one of the big schools in the East. The principal of St. Teresa's, Father Butler, was there as a teacher. Anyway we tied 1–1 so everyone felt duly proud and justified when the boys fell asleep in class on Monday and the staff looked a bit groggy.

We saw Johnny S. in Onitsha—he gave us a tour of Onitsha. He teaches physics and math at Christ the King College. He wants to build a boat 34 feet long, load his motorcycle on it, and sail around the world when he finishes the Peace Corps. He has an enormous red beard, which does make him look a lot older but a little eccentric.

Since you mention San Francisco, both of Hersh's brothers are in the area at the moment. Mendel is in the Bacteriology Department of the University of California, Berkeley for the summer and David is somewhere in the area. You could look them up maybe.

Occasionally, when the fathers use the car they return it with a chicken in the trunk. We keep it in a paper bag or box until Isaiah gets around to killing it. Somehow chickens walking through the classroom don't bother me, but imagine groping around the food closet half asleep when suddenly a paper bag begins jumping up and down and crowing!

Sometimes the homework the little boys hand in is so identical, one can't resist the impression that they are copying, which everyone knows they do. So I began one class with "So I know none of you copy your homework." Choruses of "No, Madam." "No, we do not copy." "We do not copy, Madam." In the midst of this one small boy in the first row in whom the truth was too irrepressibly present, looked up at me with his enormous eyes and said, "Yes, Madam, some of the boys copied!" His classmates were furious. I suspected they copied him, as he was one of the best students!

The first day of class I asked the prefect to make me a sitting plan of each class. Gradually the boys have discovered that not only do I not know their names unless they are in their seats, but the lighting is also very poor. They move around the room. One character named George Nwabuese seems to be everywhere. I gratefully call on a hand waving at the back of the room thinking someone new has been drawn into participating—and every time it's George again! In another class it's Edward Mauko who does this!

I have just finished a blouse and skirt. I've been doing some baking—cookies, cakes, and trying things like Chicken à la King. The term ends in two weeks. I have written Lagos about the books arriving and how I can authorize them to forward them to Enugu.

Love,
Dot

Father Desmond McGlade

Father McGlade was an important part of my work in the villages. I visited him weekly, watched him interact with the people, and watched him do Sunday masses both in the church he built and out in the bush.

He lived alone about twenty-five miles north of Nsukka deep in the bush. He had been in Nigeria thirty years when I met him and spoke fluent Igbo. He was adored by the villagers and admired by fellow priests.

Back in Ireland he had twenty-two siblings. He seemed to be in constant contact with his twin sister Maureen. His father had twelve children, then his mother died, and his father remarried and had twelve more. After leaving Africa he spent several years in California where I visited him. On one visit he showed me an album he was making of his genealogy. He had discovered some family in Australia, as I remember.

Sometimes when I visited him in Enugu Ezike (where he lived) there would be a line of people waiting to talk to him. They obviously felt he was very wise and compassionate.

"Fada, this man stole my chickens. What should I do?"

"Fada, My wife won't make any more babies. What should I do?"

"Fada, this is my son who is a bad boy. Can you talk to him?"

Sometimes other fathers would be visiting. If there was a meal, I would join them. It was usually chicken curry and rice. It was clear they enjoyed and admired him and delighted in talking about his various projects.

For example, one night it was raining very hard. Father Des felt he had to capture some of the clear, safe rainwater. So he climbed to the top of his church and created a funnel, directing the water into a barrel or some large container. He assumed he was alone and everyone was asleep. He was completely naked. But he had forgotten about the lightning. It lit up the sky for some minutes as if it was broad daylight.

He could easily have been struck by the lightning. The villagers loved hearing the story.

I went with Father one Sunday to see him say mass in the villages. We walked through one village where he met Joseph whom he had married to Mary. Mary was standing holding a baby and so were some other women. Father asked Joseph who the other women were. "Fada, these are my pagan wives. You said we should have only one Christian wife!"

Father prepared a simple altar on a table with a tablecloth and candles. There was no place to sit.

All the time he was chanting, there were a group of people pushing to get as close to him as possible, bending over him. They seemed eager to absorb every move he made. I asked him afterward who they were. He said, "Oh, those are the pagans. No one comes to see them. They are just bored!"

When he said mass in his church, thousands sat on benches, mesmerized. How they loved the cadence of Latin. They would echo his words, adding a melody and rhythm. "In nomine Dei …"

"*In no … mine ne De…i,*" they would echo, clapping their hands. The joyful sounds of their singing has lingered in my memory for fifty years.

"Et pax vobiscum …"

"*Et pax vo … bis cum!…*"

I would feel hands touching my hair which fascinated them. Or hands touching my skin to see if the white came off. They wore white chalk on their faces and hands. Father told me they thought it was beautiful to be white and were trying to be.

Later boys walked up and down the aisles waving incense lamps. Father walked back and forth, making the most of the pageantry.

He hired Israeli engineers to dig for water. I believe he was able to get some financing from Germany. They worked for weeks, and finally it happened. The children were let out of school to watch clean water gush out of the ground. A water tank was built so the women could simply line up and fill their jugs instead of walking ten miles each way every day carrying jugs on their heads (and babies tied to their backs). There was a big ceremony with the bishop of Lagos to christen it "Father McGlade's Borehole." The village gave him the most precious gift possible, a whole basket of eggs. But they were rotten and smelled nauseatingly. Whew!

I took photos of the ceremony and made him a little photo album. When I saw him in California many years later, he showed me the album. He had carried it with him always and treasured it. I was very moved.

When the war in Biafra developed in 1968, Father McGlade organized the Holy Ghost fathers and Peace Corps volunteers in rescuing children. They created a makeshift airport in the jungle. Renegade pilots flew from Fernando Po and São Tomé to bring food and take as many children out as possible. After Biafra, the Holy Ghost fathers and the Peace Corps were banned from Nigeria, as the government felt they had prolonged the war.

When I saw Father in California he still had a piece of shrapnel lodged in his spine from an incident that happened during the war. But he walked tirelessly the hills of San Francisco. He was remarkable.

Letter of July 16, 1962

… We had a most wonderful day yesterday. We went to visit Father McGlade, who lives the furthest out of all the Holy Ghost fathers—in the East. Eight years ago he moved into Enugu Ezike—the most heavily populated area of West Africa (next to Ibadan) with millions of people. They had never seen a white man before and how lucky they were that their first contact should be him. In the first four years, he built forty-six schools. Then the government forbid the Catholic fathers to build more.

He is still building in the villages where none of the Nigerian ministers would ever go to investigate. First he must build roads, the people have no idea of how to do it—and bridges are of even greater astonishment. Ninety percent of his effort is to get the people to work. They never have, and rebel at the thought of even lifting a shovel.

Then he persuades them to build a school—again, they want it but don't know how to do it, and don't immediately see the efficacy of a little effort.

We went to Eke yesterday where mostly Igala and Idomo people live. They had never seen a white woman before and never seen any other white man except Father. He is truly marvelous, built them a road and now they charge the Igbos for using it. He tells them how to stop the Igbos from cutting their valuable timber—they didn't know it was valuable. He swims and plays with them. He has built them a small school with one teacher—a fourteen-year-old boy who is the only educated person in the village.

They are all anxious to learn Igbo. The Igbos have only come into the region since Father has been here. The Igbos supply the skills—carpenters, drivers, for example. The other tribes have no skills. Father had just brought in some pipes and derricks to drill water holes. It was a fascinating day …

Water was collected in clay vats formed into the surface of the terrain

St. Teresa's College 63

Father McGlade and villagers drill for water

Villagers watch the drilling for water

Chiefs of the region watch the drilling for water

Duodecimals

I announced that I would meet with boys at St. Teresa's who were interested in singing. Sixty boys showed up. About twelve stayed with me and learned songs that we sang at assemblies during the year that followed. I thought "duodecimal" sounded like twelve and would be a good name for the group.

We met one evening a week. The boys had rich deep voices. It felt sometimes like listening to twelve Paul Robesons. They could easily have been in their twenties, as there were no records of births and deaths kept in the bush. No one knew how old they were.

Since they could not read music, I would sing a song and they would sing it back to me. Songs in which I sang a line and they answered me worked very well. Rounds were too difficult. Trying to sing different words and melodies at the same time didn't work. I listened to records like The Kingston Trio, Joan Baez, and others to get ideas.

Working with my little chorus was a real joy.

Dorothy directs the Duodecimals

Letter of July 20, 1962

… I worked hard with my chorus of sixty-four boys last night. They are growing more and more sensitive to harmonies, rhythms, and catch the words immediately now. They are a delight to work with. We have had four rehearsals and after two more, we will give a term end concert. This will be combined with some staff talent and a preview of a play they are working on—*Julius Caesar.*

I hope some of the university community will come, although with the university on vacation only a few are around.

If you could find a book of Stephen Foster songs and Christmas carols, the most popular ones, it would be truly marvelous. I intend to keep the chorus going even though I will be at the university. Maybe I will try to start a chorus at the university …

Letter or July 31, 1962

Dear Folks,

Yesterday both the shoes you mailed by air and the package of Durrell books and Spanish books arrived. Hersh was thrilled and I love the shoes. Thank you very much. It's wonderful getting mail here and the packages—well, you can't imagine!

Exams are almost over and as soon as they are we are going to travel south to Calabar and Port Harcourt. Then we have to return in time to grade another entrance exam for St. Teresa's. Then we want to go north probably as far as Lake Chad and return via Cameroun.* Although Cameroun is independent, there isn't any request for visas or papers right now.

Did you get my letter talking about a student from Ibadan we had for a dinner guest one night last week? Well, we met him at a dance ending a convention of Nigerian students. He had just been elected International Vice President of the National Convention of Nigerian students and he and other leaders had just signed another petition condemning the Peace Corps. We were shocked and asked him how he could he do it. Of course he said it was not his responsibility but the decision of the Convention. That is the usual reply to any questions on why anyone does anything in Nigeria.

(Aba used to tell me he wasn't responsible for his stories even though he was the editor—the Lagos office was....)

At any rate, after signing the petition condemning the Peace Corps as spies and attempting to indoctrinate youth with American ideas, apparently it also says that they feel the PCVs will tell the truth about Nigeria when they go home. We haven't seen this published yet. We have only heard about it from David (our guest). Hersh says that David once told him in Ibadan that anyone who wasn't slightly left was nobody in student politics. This is probably true and also of course a political movement needs something to build its definition around, to build hostility, etc. The PC offer an image which proclaims their independence, but also proves they are not taking sides in the cold war. Ah well!

One hundred PCVs are now training at UCLA and are to arrive here in September sometime. Harvard wasn't given another group to train, to everybody's surprise. Apparently the program at Harvard was not intense enough—a little too much of the studied casual approach, which Harvard does so well. I think it will take some time yet but it is coming. Harvard is falling from its pedestal s-l-o-w-l-y. UCLA struggled very hard with its program—UCLA is only thirty years old and is very keen to become one of the top five. It is already in the top ten. Training the PCVs developed their African Studies program, attracted staff and foreign students, and possibly some of the PCVs will return there for graduate work.

We met two PCVs from Sierra Leone who were on their vacation. There are about thirty-five of them and since most of the country's secondary schools are in the capital city, Freetown, fourteen of them are in Freetown. The country is little bigger than Rhode Island.

Love,
Dot

*Cameroun constitutes most of the territory of the Republic of Cameroon.

Letter from Hershel of July 31, 1962

Dear Mr. and Mrs. Crews,

The package containing The Alexandria Quartets and Look and Learn Spanish arrived yesterday. The Spanish book is exactly what I wanted. I think these books will hold us for a while, as I am also working on German and Igbo. Many thanks for your thoughtfulness.

Today was a rather unusual day in Nsukka because we had a solar eclipse. The light turned a bluish-gray and stars could be seen midday. Dottie and I hurriedly smoked a piece of glass and were able to look directly at the eclipse. Isaiah, our steward, told us that there was consternation in the market and a few of the women bolted out of their stalls yelling about Judgment Day and the end of the world.

Dottie and I have been busy making examinations and correcting them. The last day of exams will be Thursday and the boys will leave the compound for their holidays. We will leave Monday the 6th for Calabar, the old slave port and later the site of the first missionary activities in Nigeria. We hope to visit some PCVs along the way. Vanchey, our Indian friend and neighbor will join us, as he has not traveled much since coming to Africa.

We will be returning to Nsukka for about four days during which we will invigilate a school entrance examination and help with the correcting. Then it's off to the North by way of Jos, Zaria, Kaduna and Kano. From Kano we plan to drive to Maidugri and Fort-Lamy in Chad. We'll be staying in bush rest houses along the way where there are no other accommodations. A bush rest house is Nigerian for a crude building with no amenities such as water, electricity, etc. We'll take supplies, sleeping bags, and nets, with us and only stay in one as a last resort. We have been told by PCVs who have returned from the area that between Kano and Fort-Lamy the wildlife is spectacular. Elephants, baboons, hippopotami are a few of the animals we anticipate seeing.

Last week Dottie and I again went to Father McGlade's parish in the area of Enugu Ezike. We saw some of the water boreholes that he is drilling for the people. With contributions from Catholic churches in West Germany. One borehole we inspected will save the indigenous people a daily walk for fifteen miles for one pot of water. Government spending tends to be minimal in those areas that do not have ministers or parliamentarians as educated and powerful native sons. Since Enugu Ezike is one of the last areas to be opened by missionaries, it has few if any native men educated beyond standard six, which is equivalent to our first six years of primary school. Again Dot was a source of interest among the ladies of the community who had never seen a white woman.

Hersh

Letter of August 13, 1962

Dear Folks,

We have just come back from a most glorious trip to Port Harcourt, Aba, Ikot Ekpene, and Calabar. It was the first either of us had been south of Enugu and seen all of the PCVs. With the thirty PCVs coming to the Eastern Region early in September soon no one will know anyone—right now we seem like a small family. Anyway we are sending packages of carvings home, now that we have bought more. We found the shipping charges are not bad and things do really arrive.

Also I have seen what happens to slides in this climate. I can buy desiccators to absorb the moisture but nothing stops the mold. It's just terrible and once it gets on the slides it can't be removed. I've taken lots of pictures now of water holes Father McGlade is drilling—supported by parishioners in West Germany. I'm going to buy a Minolta slide projector this week. It is inexpensive and wonderful to look at the pictures.

The pictures I am sending home are:

Asaba. A Federal Training College I visited with Miss Henshaw whom I was living with at Queens before my house was ready. We stayed at the guest house, which is beautiful and at the top of a hill. There were two American missionaries who had worked in India. She is a medical doctor and he is an agricultural specialist especially invited to set up a chicken farm at Asaba. He was raising three thousand in incubators and about five hundred in cages that were laying eggs. Asaba is in the Western Region on the other side of the Niger River from Onitsha. I think I've told you about the Asaba ferry before.

Queens Athletics. This was a track meet, shot put, javelin throw between the houses at Queens. The photos of the javelin throw show the clouds. The clouds over Africa are breathtaking. The bottle race is where the girls race with bottles on their heads—they do this from the time they are small. They can run very fast with them! Erne Osora is the senior Nigeria staff member. She will probably be headmistress next year when Mrs. Kirk leaves.

Women's Athletics. All of the schools in the Eastern Region compete and then meet in Enugu with teams from the other regions. It is held in a different region each year.

Oji River. Gwen and I went to a celebration commemorating the founding of the leper colony at Oji River. They had dancing in the afternoon and a demonstration of diet, health habits, and what leprosy is. They know a considerable amount about the disease now. The slides of the dancing are not good because they were some of the first I took and I thought the sun was so bright that the lens opening should be smaller! The dancing was some of the best I have seen in Nigeria. There were groups of Igbos from the surrounding towns. It was significant that they would come to a leper colony at all … a few years ago no one would come near it. One of the groups was the patients themselves. They were very good.

Each group wore different colors. In the stilt dancing a man was on stilts about twenty feet high. The people held up Juju (magic) symbols to keep him from falling. He danced for about forty-five minutes. Quite a display.

Rogo. Some pictures of the fishing villages on the ocean. Le Benin is the hotel where we stayed. The monument was built at the time of independence in 1961. It is very beautiful, built in the French style. It is at the end of a beautifully landscaped boulevard and as you approach it, it seems to grow!

Lagos. The picture is of the little man taking our pictures for the visas to Dahomey. He fascinated me because his camera was a wooden box. After taking a picture he attached it to the front of the box and took a picture of the picture.

Ibadan University. This year the university has divorced itself from the English universities and become the first "Nigerian" university. It is truly stunning in architecture and its degrees are fully recognized.

Nsukka. This is the main square. The only building a one room post office with some children in front of it.

Father McGlade. With Hershel in front of the house he built for himself in the bush.

Oguta. I went with one of the teachers to visit. Her father has a rubber plantation, chicken farm, and other things (a Rolls-Royce!) One picture is of Papa Nwapa. As I stood on the balcony of the house and tried to take a picture of the kids going to school, they stopped and watched me.

Love,
Dot

Letter of August 19, 1962

Dear Folks,

Some of the Americans are telling me this afternoon that mail and even telegrams have gotten lost so I really wonder how many of mine do you have—it should be about a hundred I think. I mentioned in my last letter that we sent you a box. The two ebony heads are Hausa and I have been using them as bookends. I hope the fish lamp can be useful but it is a nice little decoration as is. Anyway I hope it all gets there—probably about the middle of October. I understand there is no duty on carvings coming into the country.

Our trip was wonderful. We were the first finished with correcting exams. We went with Vancheewaren, the teacher from India who lives next door, and one of his friends. We spent the first night with some friends of theirs in Port Harcourt. We met some PCVs and saw a crowd of them off on a ship *African Grove,* bound for Liberia. They were going to advise the new group of PCVs arriving in February. Actually, there are faster ways to go to Liberia. This ship started in Lagos, then to Port Harcourt, then to Cameroun, and then heading for Liberia. But for a lovely vacation as well!

We found a marvelous restaurant. After driving 185 miles through impoverished villages, we came suddenly upon a beautiful structure lit with colored lights. We hopped out of the car and learned it was Silver Valley Roadhouse … air-conditioning, soft music, carpets. Furthermore they wouldn't serve us because the men had no jackets on. The dining room was set with white linen tablecloths, silverware, had waiters dressed formally in black … but *no* customers! It was too bizarre for words.

Finally the headwaiter produced two jackets and we sat down to a meal of wine, steak, turtle soup, and real coffee!

We spent the next night in Aba because we wanted to see the film playing in town—*Ali Baba and the Forty Thieves*—it featured Fernandel as Ali Baba. It was a delightful show in an outdoor theater with a curved balcony.

Then we went to Calabar. We left the car at the police station in Oran on the west side of the Cross River. Then we took an hour-and-a-half trip by ferry to Calabar. Calabar was once the capital of the Eastern Region and a bustling city. Now that Cameroun is no longer part of Nigeria, Calabar is gradually dying. Only one ferry a day from the Nigerian side. Smugglers bring in liquor from a Spanish island on the coast. The smuggler is as regular a visitor as the Hausa traders. There are three PCVs in Calabar. They place their orders for brandy, etc. with their regular smuggler. They are stationed at Hope Wadell, one of the oldest and finest boys schools. Their house is beautiful on cement legs with a porch that looks down on a lawn dotted with palm trees reaching to the sea. They have two motor scooters for the three of them and ride all their guests around. Wonderful trip!

Love,
Dot

Letter of August 31, 1962

Dear Folks,

We've just spent a marvelous four days traveling to Ibadan and Lagos. We drove straight through to Ibadan, spent the day, and then drove to Lagos. Our Indian friends had never seen an escalator before and it was delightful to run around a big department store with them! It seems so wonderful to be back in civilization again.... Air-conditioning! Steaks and special deserts! Milk! What that must taste like to a Nigerian. There is a Nigerian on St. Teresa's staff who just returned from ten tears in America with an American wife. He feels he has been thoroughly spoiled and becomes quickly impatient and discouraged by Nigeria.

We bought sweaters, skirts, dresses for me, some records, books, a slide projector. We saw the Houses of Parliament. They were opened in August 1959 and were really beautiful—designed by a German architect and with wood carvings by a Nigerian. It reminded me of the United Nations building inside. Modern architecture and furniture is perfectly legitimate for Africa. Since Africa never went through the various styles of European and Oriental worlds, the functional, elegant lines of modern architecture are perfect here.

We saw an Indian movie in Ibadan—quite a production. Very imaginative, complicated, almost whimsical plot, versatile actors, warm and perceptive relationships, but not always logical. At a critical moment, the actors would break into a romantic song—delightful but not logical!

We were gone five days. Isaiah had waxed the floor with red polish, which wasn't exactly what we wanted but he had worked so hard we got very excited over it. Tomorrow Father Butler wants us to drive to Enugu to meet two more staff members from Ireland. The man has been here before, but they have just gotten married and are coming for their honeymoon!

Love,
Dot

Letter of September 1, 1962

... THE BOOKS HAVE COME!!!!

They are snuggled quietly in the storeroom at Queens College. The crates are in perfect condition and look brand new. I can go down there tomorrow....

Sewing Projects

Driving through the bush and visiting markets, I saw beautiful materials with colorful exotic patterns. There were also men working on sewing machines. The women wore pieces of cloth wrapped around themselves, called "wrappers." Rarely did one see a dress styled and sewn from a pattern. Women never wore pants, and neither did we. So I thought girls in the villages might like to learn how to sew their own dresses.

Father McGlade told me where to find the villages. There were no road signs, or names of roads or villages anywhere. I would just know to drive when the road forked and then turn left. I usually went to the schoolhouse. Now I realize it was probably a school Father had built.

I had one dress pattern, which I cut out of plastic so it would not tear. I would hold it up to the girl and adjust it, then pin it to the material and cut. Then cut the rest of the pieces, holding them up to show what I was doing. Then I would begin to sew them together by hand. I used as few words as possible. Using a needle and thread was a new experience, but they caught on quickly. I would work with a few girls, leave pieces of material and thread, and explain I would come back next week.

Each week the number of interested girls grew. One day when I was cutting out a piece for a dress, a breast dangled in front of me. The woman wanted to see what I was doing. More and more women came, as well as girls. I smiled at her and continued cutting—very carefully.

When I drove into the bush, I would stop and visit Father McGlade. He wasn't always there as he was busy building another big church as well as looking after the villagers.

When I began teaching at the university, I still kept going to the villages and creating sewing projects.

About February 1963, Queen of the Rosary, a school run by the Sisters for girls, asked me to create a sewing class for them. Brigid, the British volunteer teaching with me at the university, helped me with this class. The girls were all using the same pattern, but added bows, sashes, or did the skirts differently. Their dresses all had an individual touch. At the end we held a style show. I had teachers, some from the university, and Elizabeth, a World Health Organization nurse, as judges. There were twenty-five girls and they won prizes. The judges looked at their stitches, hems, and how well they fit.

Since the Style Show was on April 4, I have included the program later in this book.

Letter of September 1, 1962

… The sewing projects have mushroomed. I hope it doesn't absorb all our money—they have cut salaries because some people were able to save too much money—mostly those living in isolated areas where they couldn't spend it if they had to. But everyone had a cut …

Letter of September 6, 1962

… I have been going out to the bush every day this week. About ten little girls have started blouses. Some should finish on Friday. About twenty-five girls showed up from another village and they all want to make skirts. Tomorrow I must buy about fifty yards of material at the market—two yards per skirt. I charge 5 shillings for a skirt and 3 for a blouse, and 9 for a dress. I have to start some dresses next week. Then I want to have a fashion show, maybe with music and commentary while the girls model the clothes they made …

Letter of September 12, 1962

… They would pay that much for the material alone and that much at least if they wanted to have them made for them …

Letter of September 22, 1962

… One sewing project is about finished—about forty to fifty little girls made skirts and blouses. I have some material left, which I hope to sell. I am going to another village Monday and hope they will want to make dresses. It is better to have a style show where they have made matching skirts and blouses. I have designed another type of dress, which I hope they will make …

In a Little Newsletter Called The Tille Lamp

"Through some fathers who have built schools and churches throughout the bush around Nsukka, I have become very familiar with the countryside. I went into one of Father's schools—a primary school, Enugu-Ezike—and began a sewing class with about thirty girls, nine to fifteen years old. I underestimated their enthusiasm and only brought material for sixteen skirts, which they have now finished. I'll buy material in Enugu and charge them a few shillings for each skirt. Next they want to make blouses and school uniforms … little white dresses!"

Letter of November 1, 1962

… Anyway I have begun another sewing project. This time it is at the Health center with a group of women of assorted ages who are practicing midwives. They are supported by their local councils to complete a course in public health nursing. They are a somewhat more sophisticated group to work with and on the whole rather disagreeable. They bought material from me and apparently thought that was what I was there for. I'm going back next week to see if they seriously want to sew.

Then today I went to Unadu, which I started last Tuesday. I was not able to go out last Thursday. There was no one there. They thought I wouldn't come. I was sort of annoyed and told them if they could not come, neither could I. I drove to Father's house to tell him. He will talk to them. We will see what happens. Father feels that the people are feeling increasingly confident and bold towards him. Possibly this will get worse, not better. Most people predict that within five years the white Catholic fathers will have left. Certainly they are constantly reminded that their days are numbered …

Letter of November 8, 1962

… Went out to Unadu this week and *this* time everything went very well. About ten blouses are being made and the girls were in a good mood! Brigid is good and she is going to begin her own project next week in another village if Father can arrange it. (Brigid is the English volunteer who is teaching French with me at the university) …

Letter of November 17, 1962

Dear Folks,

The days are getting increasingly dry, cool, except for the middle of the day, and sleepy. Somehow it is harder and harder to accomplish much in a day. Brigid and I have gone out twice this week and begun one project, starting up another. These two projects promise to be the nicest so far.

The latest gossip has it that the university will open either November 26 or December 3, which leaves about ten days more. Probably each term will be extended a week. Some faculty would even complain about this.

Each trip out to a village, I usually stop and chat with Father McGlade. We were discussing superstitions. They are an integral part of the life of the people and in fact an important controlling factor. Juju statues keep people out of each other's yam patches, away from young maidens, probably avoiding those who are sick, thus not contracting contagious diseases.

One of the most powerful forces in their lives is the force of magic. If a family has had a great deal of illness or hard luck, it consults the high pagan priest. Formerly he would tell them to sacrifice one of their young daughters. Now it is considered murder, but probably still exists in places where it cannot be discovered. Now instead they take the tendons out of the legs of the girls from the knee down, leaving her nothing but stumps to walk on for the rest of her life. Father says around Owerri one can see many girls like this now. Occasionally there is one in the villages around here.

If someone steals something, the process of justice such as it is in the village, nails a nail through the head and the person is left to wander in the bush completely ostracized by everyone. Father took a nail out of a girl's head and took her to a hospital. She returned to her village, but he does not know what has become of her now.

At the time of the nuclear testing in the Sahara, one could get fallout injections in the market. One stood backwards next to a curtain from which the needle emerged. The doctor is never seen. The injection was probably water, ten shillings each! Bottles of wondrous herbs are sold listing over two hundred diseases and with this at the bottom of the labels: "If anyone is cured of a disease not listed below with this medicine, please let us know."

I have been doing some cooking lately. For example, trying soufflés, pineapple and banana fritters, shrimp Newbury, yeast coffee cake. Also doing some sewing for myself, two new dresses.

Our neighbor, the Indian education officer, is going home in a couple of weeks, and is terribly anxious about the border dispute between India and China. He may very well be conscripted. It appears that India has been rather foolish for the last eight years in supporting China's admission to the UN, letting Tibet slip, and other infringements on the India-China border, accepting feeble excuses from China for each. Now India is completely unprepared, without sufficient supplies from the West accumulated, or even capital resources allocated efficiently. This was predicted but is devastating nonetheless.

Love,
Dot

Letter of November 28, 1962

... Today I am going out sewing for the last time before January. I hope to finish up about thirteen blouses. This project at Aji has been the best so far, and I hope to develop it more after the holidays. The kids love to practice their English whenever they can. One little girl had to take out some stitching and in the process ripped her blouse.

When she showed it to Bridgid, another one leaning curiously over her shoulder said, "By God, you have ripped it and by your own hand!" Obviously conned from some old English text!!...

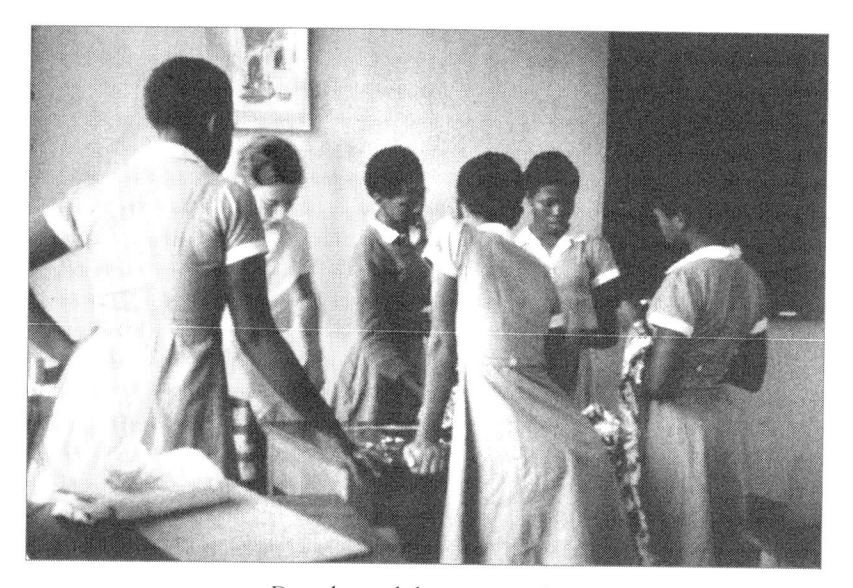

Dorothy with her sewing class

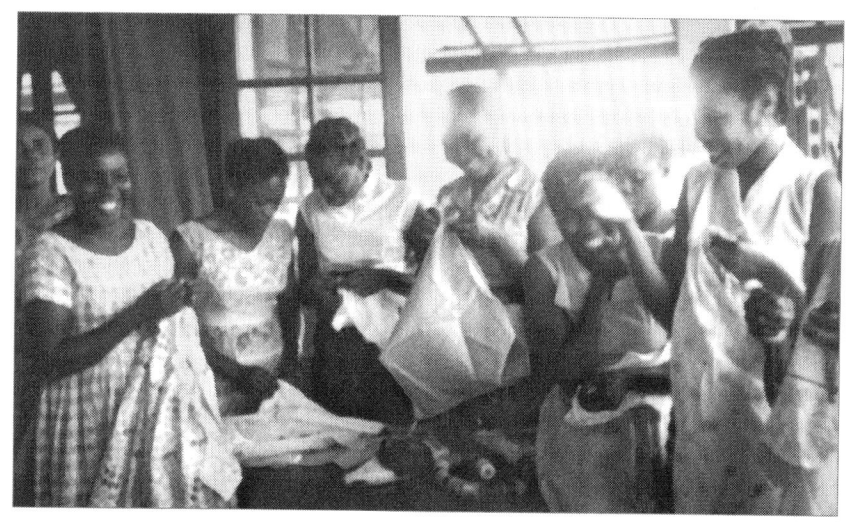

Another sewing class for nurses

When the bishop came to visit, people crowded around to kiss his ring. A little boy stepped forward wearing nothing but a small red hat. A priest stepped out and spoke to him telling him that if he wanted to kiss the bishop's ring, he would have to remove his hat.

Juju was a traditional ritual in which someone dressed in a costume covering his face. It was forbidden to know who was under the costume. Even if the villagers knew, they could not say. The dancer spun and jumped around and around to drums. Villagers watched quietly. The juju dancer would appear or disappear unexpectedly.

Juju dancer

The University of Nigeria (pictured above in 2013) is an indigenous, autonomous university, modeled on the U.S. educational system

University of Nigeria, Nsukka

Perspectives on Nigerian History

I found that the more deeply I became immersed in Nigeria, my perspective on its experience as a British colony changed radically. In the two years I was there, there were many opportunities to talk with thoughtful, educated Nigerians. Never once did I hear anyone complain about being a British colony, nor about Englishmen, nor about learning English history, reading English literature, or having British district officers (DOs) living throughout the bush. For almost two years after independence the district officers stayed on. I would see a long line waiting every afternoon at 4:00 p.m. outside the district office for Nsukka. People wanted advice and help, and the DO was always patient and receptive.

I came to Nigeria with a college major and master's degree in history. My courses had numerous descriptions and discussions of the horrors of colonialism. I expected to find contempt for colonialism. Colonialism had destroyed indigenous culture. Colonialism was brutal and insensitive. Colonialism imposed Western custom. One example of this was naming the days of the week. Nigerians referred to market day, the day before market day, two days after market day, etc. as their way of managing time. Or the custom of serving tea every afternoon. Only in the British colonies was this introduced.

During the one hundred years that England governed Nigeria, roads were built, railroads were built, airports and airplanes and harbors were built. A civil service system was established in which jobs were filled by exams instead of patronage and nepotism. Government schools were established and missionary schools supported. Nigerians went to universities in England, Scotland, France, Germany, Australia, and the United States. When they came back speaking several languages they were dubbed "been tos" and were expected to support every single relative. The been tos were expected to live in a large house and their aunts and uncles, cousins, second cousins, third cousin, etc. moved in.

Nigerian women did not wear slacks and neither did we. Nigerian men could choose to wear western dress or African. Many of the been tos wore blue serge suits even in the tropical heat. If the been to brought back an expatriate wife, her first meeting with his family living in the bush was traumatic. Any child born to a Nigerian in Nigeria belonged to the Nigerian citizen. If the wife attempted to take the child back to her country, she would be stopped at the airport, on the plane if necessary.

The British were deeply respected and admired by Nigerians. Outside their legislature in Lagos is a huge statue of Queen Elizabeth II.

Recently when I entered a history class in a high school where I was substituting, I was handed some worksheets on Nigeria I was to give the students. The worksheet read, "The British left Nigeria without developing a mid-level workforce." This was explained as office workers, administrators, etc. Apparently the story now is that the British did not do *enough*.

History changes depending on who is telling the story, and when.

Letter of September 16, 1962

... The whole university faculty—one hundred of us—discussed problems of registration today. I have an office and schedule, and classes start in two weeks. The students arrive now but are issued only temporary rooms and meal tickets. Next week they take the scholarship exams and for many of them if they don't survive that they will have to leave. Probably half or less can pay their own way. They are admitting five hundred students this year and in June will have their first graduating class. I am very happy to be on the faculty and hope I can continue something like it when I get home ...

Letter of September 27, 1962

Dear Folks,

First let me say I read your last letter and I note some misunderstanding; the salary cut was not so disastrous and the sewing projects are not driving us broke. I included such items only as news; please don't exaggerate.

I am sending you more slides and here is a description of them:

Some Peace Corpsmen. They are standing outside my house at Queens before the group left for Kaduna. Some at Ife where they are stationed. One at Onitsha where Johnny S is and we visited him one day.

Asaba Ferry. This is the boat across the Niger River from Onitsha. You drive down a sloping road onto the ferry and on the other side you back off up a very steep incline. Every time one thinks they aren't going to make it.

Western House of Assembly. This was taken the day after there were bloody riots in the House. If one hadn't read the papers, one would never have known anything had happened!

Ife. This was right outside the museum where the famous bronze statues of Ife are. No one knows who created these pieces. They are very sophisticated—Greek-like in concept—found buried in this square where the pieces are playing chess.

Murray Frank. He is the Peace Corps representative in the Western Region. He was working in social work in White Plains somewhere and said the name "Crews" seemed familiar.

Onitsha. The biggest market in West Africa. Unfortunately it was Sunday and it was closed the day we took these pictures.

Ibadan. Ibadan University is Nigeria's first university. The architecture is stunning and puts Nsukka to shame. Its standards are almost those of a British university. It has a beautiful hospital and a medical school, law school, etc.

Togo and Dahomey.* Taken in May. The road goes along the ocean and right beside little fishing villages and fishing shacks on stilts. The cities of Cotonou and Lomé are different from British West Africa in the landscaping of the roads—lined with palm trees.

Father McGlade's Church. He designed it and built it himself. Neither he nor the workers had ever done anything like it before. It holds some two thousand people. He gives the sermon in Igbo and English, and the singing, or rather, Latin chanting, with Igbo intonations is very moving.

Tomorrow we register our classes. Next Thursday is convocation when the chancellor—the Honorable Nnamdi Azikiwe, governor general of Nigeria will be present.

Love,
Dot

*Dahomey is now Benin.

Letter of September 30, 1962

Dear Folks,

The records came! They are beautiful and in perfect condition. Thank you very much; they are absolutely irreplaceable. I've been asking people if there are any such records around the university and no one seems to know. There are many staff members who want to take French lessons and one of us is going to end up doing it. Hersh has begun his German lessons and is quite excited about it.

We have been registering students at the university for the last three days. All the French sections have filled up and we had to create two more. With the same size staff as last year, we now have to cope with five sections of beginning French, in addition to five sections of second year French. The department is wonderful and actually we think it is the best in the university—all young and about my age except for the chairman who is a lively Irishman and delightful. The major occupation of the faculty seems to be gossiping and already I am absorbed in this. Unfortunately, the university is too busy investing in buildings, salaries, dormitories, etc. to pay anybody to do research.

As much as we complain about the pressure of research on the faculty in the States, the lack of it here produces a kind of mental laziness.

At any rate, if everyone were totally engrossed in research, a totally different atmosphere would prevail. It is stimulating nonetheless to see a huge university unfold. The students are quite bright and eager to learn anything and everything. They will of course be the leaders of tomorrow and are already the top ten percent of the population at their present level of education.

The atmosphere is closer, warmer, and more supportive than in a settled university in some aspects. For instance, everyone is called upon to do everything. So the same people are in the university band, chorus, orchestra, plays, etc. Someone who came to teach something finds himself singing Radamès in *Aida*! All the secretaries and administrators are part of the big family. On the whole, everyone mixes well. There are several mixed marriages, English and Nigerian, German and Nigerian, Indian and American ...

The administrators are American Negroes and some seem to be very happy here.

I am going to a mass at Father McGlade's church.

Love,

Dot

Letter of October 4, 1962

Dear Folks,

The language records came and they are wonderful. We listened to part of them and I am going to type out some pages of the manual to be mimeographed for my students to follow the record. Since you enjoyed the newspapers so much, I will try to send more. I found at first I read them carefully, but now we never look at them—partly because we have the news every morning on the radio, but also because the best accounts of the world news are in the Western papers when we get a chance to see them.

Today was the convocation at the university. Last night some members of the Peace Corps were sitting in our house having dinner.

They realized they could not march in the procession because none of them had robes. So I got up at 6:00 a.m. this morning and drove to Enugu and borrowed four robes from the staff of Queens College. We got back (one of then went with me) with fifteen minutes to spare; I ran home, changed, and was in time to photograph them in the procession!

The ceremony was held in one of the big auditoriums and the Honorable Nnamdi Azikiwe (Zik), the chancellor of the university, was present. He is quite a charming, brilliant man and gave a one-and-a-half-hour address. He outlined first the names of each college within the university and the colorful lives of the people for which each is named. Then he welcomed the students and *then* he made some remarks about the Peace Corps. He described how he had flown G. Mennen Williams to Nsukka in his private plane. He told how he had discussed sending thirty PCVs to Nsukka with Sargent Shriver in Washington. He mentioned that he offered to pay them regular salaries in addition to what they received from the American government. He neglected to mention this had not been done. He stressed they should be treated as guests of Nigeria and the misdemeanors of a few individuals should not be taken as reason to condemn the whole project. All in all, the air cleared considerably and I think everyone was surprised and pleased.

Certainly I hope now the students will no longer think of the Peace Corps as their own private political football. All of the Nsukka group were radiant as it made all of last year's frustrations worthwhile. I think this year they will enjoy things much more. The ones who wore the robes in the procession were also pleased.

Afterwards, there was a reception for Zik in the Rest House and the whole faculty was there. I met him twice—he is a most vital presence. And tonight I came straight back for a chorus rehearsal for a concert Sunday.

Hersh is working hard at German classes, cataloging the new books for the library, inspection and other responsibilities of being a dorm master, opening a sickroom (he will be the first patient; he has sprained his foot today playing basketball), and finding speakers for his current events club. The current events club is most interesting. He has met with it several times and the boys discuss anything that has been in the news. This is quite a novelty here, as they study ancient history and Victorian literature but never anything since 1918. Even in the university they are reluctant to sign up for modern history for some reason.

Love,
Dot

Letter of October 21, 1962

... The students had rallies this week to elect officers. They were interesting; for once absolutely nothing was mentioned about the Peace Corps, so Zik's speech must have made some difference. Their gripes concentrated on house rules and complaining about the food. Since about eighty percent of them are on university scholarships, there were no complaints about the academic side—although they have many frustrations there, such as not enough French lecturers, etc. Each candidate and each incumbent stood in front of a microphone in the Margaret Ekpo Refectory and spoke to the students—about one thousand of them. (The refectory is named after Nigeria's only woman suffragette—a very successful member of the Eastern House of Assembly and quite a woman; I've met her.) The students are quick-tempered, high-strung, and easily aroused. At about 10:30 one incumbent whom the students detested was the last speaker of the event. Evidently the students had anticipated this because bedlam broke out and the faculty (Nigerian) who had been moderating, fled.

In snake dance lines they raided the girls dormitories, the girls threw them out bodily, and then they ran all over the campus. A group of PCVs who were sitting in the front of the rally were not involved at all—in fact, the students danced completely around them and even ran up to explain why they were doing it. Many of the older students walked out. Students from minority groups within the university disengaged themselves—the Yoruba and Hausa students for example. The university is largely Igbo—whether anyone admits it or not—when another university opens in the West and in the North, the Yoruba and Hausa would much prefer to go to them. They do not wish to irritate or enrage the hostilities which already exist—apparently they are made painfully aware they are Yoruba and Hausa.

The students, like most Nigerians, are much more confident and articulate about what they are against rather than what they are for. They cannot envision what they would do if they were in authority so do not offer any concrete alternatives.

Nigerians who seem best to understand the workings of a democracy are those who have been to America or England—they cannot learn it in Nigeria apparently.

Love,
Dot

Letter of October 26, 1962

Dear Folks,

I have at the moment a bad cold and malaria which is very common and nothing to be concerned about—which, however, accentuates all the moods of homesickness. But the news of Cuba is most disconcerting. The students are curious about it—they live it chiefly through us since it seems very remote to them. From what I can gather from the BBC, newspapers, and word of mouth, everyone seems happy that Kennedy did something at last. The support of the OAS* means a lot for American prestige. It sees now if they will not bring this before world opinion in the UN, it will reduce the UN to nothing overnight. It would seem that Kennedy has called the Russian's bluff, but the thing might dribble on for years, as in Berlin, with Russians ducking all attempts to discuss it. What are the Cuban people doing? How angry are the OAS states? What would happen if UN members materially supported the blockade thus forcing Russia to discuss it?

Many of the Indian community here are worried about the India-China fighting. What has Krishna Menon† said on it?

How are the elections? I know you are probably deeply involved in them—who is running for what?

I am trying to organize an Alliance Francaise on campus and had the first meeting with a small committee yesterday. We are writing everywhere to find material on France. I am taking the language records down this morning to find a portable phonograph somewhere. Heaven knows if the library is really putting their records on tape.

I went out to a new village this week to begin more blouses and dresses. I had a charming WHO‡ nurse (Elizabeth) with me. She has been here a year training Nigerian nurses and running a health center.

The health center now has a Russian on the staff. He has a wife and daughter with him and none of them speak anything but Russian. They are not aggressive or offensive in any way but they are adamant and somewhat defensive on the principles of their great revolution. They refuse to hire servants and do all the marketing and cooking themselves on a cumbersome wood stove. They walk everywhere and refuse to socialize with anyone. From what anyone can gather, he was quite a successful doctor at home and is terribly impatient with his inability to communicate and do anything here. He is trying to learn English.

Elizabeth wants me possibly to take a group of young mothers who come to the health center and teach them sewing—and then possibly the nurses also. She is trying to get them to begin kinds of community centers when they go back to their villages, perhaps teach sewing themselves. We shall sew …

Love,

Dot

*Organization of American States (The Americas)

†V. K. Krishna Menon was an important diplomat and statesman of India.

‡World Health Organization (United Nations)

Student Riots: University in Nsukka

Letter of November 1, 1962
Student Strike

... Things have been bustling around here. Yesterday in the middle of my 12:00 class, a group of students began chanting somewhere on campus. The noise grew and some of my students jumped up and ran out to join. I asked what it was and they explained it was a strike against the high-handedness of the administration and against the bad food. I finished the lesson and released the students about fifteen minutes early and they went out to join the crowd.

Students began singing an Igbo version of "Solidarity Forever," then chanting, and increasingly angry. They marched through the catwalks of the administration building and through the offices, and finally threw rocks through the windows at the staff inside. By this time they were about five hundred strong. They marched up the hill to the dean's office. They didn't find him in so they marched to the office of the assistant dean (Nigerian). They did quite a bit of damage to his car—slit tires, smashed windows. They tried to break into his apartment and frightened his wife.

I was standing in the driveway of the house next door. Then they ran past and on to Chukwudebe's house. He is Zik's representative on campus. The five hundred or so in front were quite angry, running and chanting, but the ones behind were just high-spirited, waving and shouting, *"Bonjour, Madame!"*

They threw flowerpots through all the windows of Chukwudebe's house. He was in Lagos for a meeting of the University Council, which is a body that coordinates financial support to all three Nigerian universities—Ife, Ibadan, and Nsukka. The vice chancellor, Dr. Johnson, an American Negro—was also at the meeting.

Previous to looking for the dean's house, they had wreaked havoc in the refectory, breaking china, glasses, tables, and damaging some of the machinery. They found the house of the woman who runs it and tore through it, breaking everything. They would probably have attacked her if she had been there. They beat up some of the kitchen stewards who of course have nothing to do with anything.

The district officer was called. He has the authority to do anything to restore order (the same man Hersh worked with on the census). Police came and surrounded the administration building and riot police were due. Everyone expected a breakout last night and even Halloween parties were canceled. But they did nothing except bang on doors and ask for food.

Classes were canceled today and it is rumored that they will not come to class until Monday now.

The universities of Ife and Ibadan have gone on sympathy strikes. Zik has issued a furious statement from Lagos and investigations have begun prior to expelling the leaders if they can find them, which is doubtful.

The vice president of the student body is a white American from Brooklyn. He just arrived about six weeks ago. He ran on a ticket, "a vote for us is a voice against racial prejudice" and clearly stating he is not subversive and is *not* a member of the Peace Corps. He is very popular and is certainly organizing much of the activity. I believe they intended a peaceful demonstration to shake the administration but became carried away. Many American girls are in the student body—right in the thick of things.

On the whole it seems to have been directed against Nigerian members of the staff—particularly administrators. One American registrar was hissed at. Not a single white person was touched possibly because the administration that deals with the students is entirely Nigerian or American Negro. There is however a definite differentiation between Americans and other assorted Negroes, and everyone else. They feel safer taking things out on them. The faculty is furious and claims they will do something if the administration won't—I suppose that means disciplining the students. They have not eaten for two days and some are going home. This is somewhat ludicrous because what they will eat at home is a big bowl of fufu similar to what they would have eaten in the refectory.

The University Council has threatened mass expulsion. We are all going to classes as usual even if no one shows up. If the students expected to achieve popularity, probably they have failed. Everyone is ashamed and annoyed at their behavior, and probably Zik himself will come to assess the damage ...

Letter of November 3, 1962

... Yesterday Dr. Johnson—the vice chancellor—called a meeting of the faculty and administration. Some felt there were subversive or outside influences whipping up the situation. Some, mostly Nigerians, felt there was absolutely no excuse for the students' behavior and the entire student body should have been suspended immediately and the university closed for three months. Then the damage assessed and the amount added to each student's tuition, and each student carefully screened before being allowed to reenter. Some students will be expelled, but it seems obvious Dr. Johnson will not expel the whole student body. This was actually done at the University of Ibadan in 1949 when the university closed following student riots. They have had no more trouble.

The more I think about it, this seems a good solution. The students were particularly cocky in class today. They feel they have pulled off a coup and gotten away with it. They have already issued an ultimatum to some departments stating that standards are too high and why aren't there more facilities, etc. There is a feeling that there would be sympathy strikes when and if any students are dismissed.

The Nigerian staff is terrified. The students detest them for not holding their lectures (they leave for conferences, meetings of Parliament, etc.), not turning in grades—whether they feel there will be recriminations if the grades are not high. Some of the male students refuse grades from female lecturers. Students also feel some lecturers are incompetent ...

Letter of November 7, 1962
Resolution of Student Riots

Dear Folks,

First the news. Yesterday at 9:45 a.m. I was sitting in my office when the head of the department ran in with notice from the vice chancellor to all members of the staff to: 1. If they had 9:00 classes, dismiss the students at 9:50 and send them back to their hostels; 2. In view of the existing unrest for all members of the staff to return to their houses or leave the campus by 10:00; and 3. An important proclamation would be issued to the students at 10:00.

So I got in the car and left.

I went to visit some WHO people who live on a hill opposite the university and from where I could see the entire campus clearly. So we had coffee and watched. We could see nothing but long lines of lorries we supposed were police, going up to the campus and then presently moving away. About one o'clock I went back to the campus. I had told the students I would play the French records there. By that time it was all over!

All the students were expelled and the university closed. The ones who lived furthest away were taken in lorries. The others sat at Nsukka center waiting for taxis, lorries, or any way to get a ride. Riot police equipped with tear gas, shields, megaphones, marched around and stood in each dormitory (hostels as they are called) as the students packed. There was no fighting. Some were subdued, some seemed jubilant, still thinking it was a fine game. They will all reregister and will not be refunded any money for the time they are missing. The faculty seems relieved. Some PCVs have already left for Lagos to visit the trade fair.

I'm going into the bush. My sewing classes at the health center yesterday went very well indeed. They are making baby dresses and a few blouses. It seems the disagreeable few were absent.

The general feeling I think is that the university will be closed anywhere from two weeks to a month. There are only six weeks of the term left, so whether they will open it for the rest of the term no one knows. Each student will be personally written and I suppose those they don't want, not invited. If they had dismissed certain individuals, which I think they had originally planned to do, there would certainly have been riots …

Letter of November 8, 1962

… Things are strangely quiet on campus with the students gone. There is nothing to do around the department, so I think I will volunteer my services to the Cataloging Department in the library.

The president of the student body absconded with funds allotted to the Student Union. He was enormously popular among the students and detested by the faculty.…

Letter of November 13, 1962

Dear Folks,

Some of the volunteers and I went off this weekend to Aba, Ikot Ekpene, and Calabar. Hersh didn't come, as he is teaching for still another week. Our Christmas vacation might be all off if the university opens at all this term. It might stay in session longer in December, and open in January. Or it might open early in January, but at any rate we won't have more than two weeks. The university faculty is taking extended weekend trips now.

It was a wonderful trip. At the big movie theater in Aba we saw the silent film *King of Kings*. As there was no sound, the audience provided commentary—cheers when the blind girl opened her eyes and when Lazarus rose from the dead, and violent catcalls at Judas Iscariot. When the people followed Jesus instead of the High Priest, it sounded like a home-team touchdown at the Yale stadium! They all chanted the written dialogue in unison like a responsive reading. This is Protestant territory.

Then we went to Calabar. The trips on the ferry were two hours long but at cool times of day and very pleasant. My friends the two PCVs at Hope Waddell School were away so we walked all over Calabar. We walked up and down hills visiting all the churches. We got back to the rest house just before the rain. The boys had still not returned to Hope Waddell, but the principal invited us for a cup of tea after the Sunday evening service. So we met the staff and we tried to explain what had happened and why the university is closed. The students seem to be rationalizing it. It is rumored they have set up a provisional government somewhere near Enugu. Public opinion seems to be against them, however, and feels the university authority did the right thing.

Anyway, the boys finally returned and put up all five of us in their big house. We went through Ikot Ekpene market on the way back and bought masks, statues, and musical instruments. We played all the things we had bought on the way back and had quite a jam session. We came back, washed, and collected Hersh and four other PCVs, and went to a movie in Enugu last night. Wonderful time!

Love,
Dot

Language department staff and some students

Letter of November 22, 1962

Dear Folks,

I think it is most interesting that not a word of it (the university closure) was reported in the American press—it is all over the Nigerian press, including the accusations that the Peace Corps at Nsukka inspired the whole thing. Also that all the investigating and other administrative committees that have been set up are run by members of the Peace Corps. The ideas are so totally absurd as to be funny. We sat around and decided what committees we would like to head.

None of us are involved in any way with decisions made by the university authorities. Since we are not paid and none of us are higher than lecturers, there are probably 160 people whose opinions are more important than ours.

The university is opening on Monday with the students signing a pledge that they will behave themselves. Classes begin on Wednesday. No one knows what investigation has been done into their grievances although the administration frankly admits they were justified. Probably the rest of this term will be peaceful, but then what?

It seems Zik is losing popularity, as the Yoruba and Hausa are beginning to climb in Nigerian politics—places which the Igbo have occupied for years. The Igbo had no cultural heritage to fall back on when colonialism began. The Igbo were raided by other tribes and sold as slaves. It was the arrival of the missionaries, which gave the Igbo a chance. The Igbos learned skills and attended schools and took the lead in the struggle for independence. The economy is virtually controlled by the Igbos, which is becoming increasingly resented by the other tribes. The educated and some brilliant Nigerians returning are needed in politics, but are not necessarily above bribery or corruption.

It is not always easy to understand Nigerian politics!

Love,

Dot

Letter of December 7, 1962

Dear Folks,

The university has reopened and is running smoothly. Relations between faculty and administration are considerably improved and the students are calmer. Altogether the riots were perhaps the best thing that could have happened—everyone has felt for a long time that they were coming.

As soon as the students arrive, everything is back to normal—no water. Either we are the last to get water as the pipes flow first to the university, or what, I don't know, but the demand is greater than the pressure or something. The university will close on the 15th—next Saturday and then we plan to leave immediately for a trip. Dakar is really too expensive and so far that it will be exhausting. So we will probably go to Abidjan, Ivory Coast, for a while and then to Accra, Ghana. We are really keen to see Ghana.

Anyway, things are hectic. People are coming and going. Some of St. Teresa's staff have left for home leave, others are pregnant. So the whole staff practically will turn over again next term. Certainly the boys get a most fascinating view of human nature with the parade of teachers they survive. The compound is deserted and feels most strange.

I must walk down and catch a taxi to the university today, as Hersh took the car to the village he is visiting. It is not really inconvenient, as the taxis run just outside the gate. The language department is about a mile in walking distance.

Love,
Dot

Trip to Ivory Coast

Letter of December 13, 1962

… In two days we leave! Three weeks in Abidjan it will be. Our money won't stretch to Dakar, and Ghana has just come out with an anti-American campaign, so no Americans are allowed to go in or out of Ghana. This immediately affects the Peace Corps in both countries, as the Ghanaian group would be on annual leave at this time too. Some of the Peace Corps in Nsukka had already left for a Pan-African conference in Accra before this came out. Also some of the faculty who left are married to Americans, so are half Americans. At any rate, we don't know exactly what has happened but it's a good subject of conversation!

We've let the food get used up and the gas has finished. We've had no water for two weeks. And now the fathers have had the car. So I walk down and get taxis to school. This is nerve-racking, as they often have several passengers to deliver first and one never knows if it is going to make it or not. Taxis are usually cars that have been almost demolished and left or sold for junk, and then rehabilitated by some skilled Nigerian workman, naturally. They rattle around indefinitely, doors clattering, gas tanks leaking, etc. Anyway tonight we are visiting PCV friends staying in a rest house, hoping they will offer us a shower! We can always get dinner there and then a taxi back! It's such an experience to be a PCV.

Before I forget to mention it, the packages should be marked, "Educational Material"—otherwise they cost up to one third of the price or value declared on the outside—which is rather ridiculous in the case of the shoes, for instance. As educational material they cost nothing. All the PCVs here are getting shirts, fancy sausages, books, mustache clippers, etc. as educational material.…

Letter of January 9, 1963

... We left Nsukka on December 15 at 5:00 a.m. in a Peace Corps bus with five other PCVs. The driver took us to Onitsha and then brought the bus back to Nsukka. We took a ferry across and then a taxi to Benin, and then another taxi to Ibadan, arriving there about 7:00 p.m. that night. We ate at the West End Café, which is a very good restaurant run by a Syrian serving Middle Eastern food—shish kebabs, rice in grape leaves, eggplant, mashed sesame seeds spread on thin pancake-like bread. Delicious! We got a ride the next day in another PC bus to Lagos and stayed with the Peace Corps administrators there. Ran around Lagos getting visas, tickets, changing money for a couple of days, and then flew to Abidjan. We took Nigerian Airways to Accra and had to stay overnight, which we wanted to do anyway. We took a taxi around Accra and saw Black Star Square, which was interesting. A huge deserted square with an arch with a black star on top. A lonely statue of an unknown soldier and a huge paved space facing the sea. Right on the edge of the sea, an arch in a semicircle with a platform across it where supposedly Nkrumah* stands when he addresses a mob of citizens. We took several pictures but eventually a guard approached us and said we were not supposed to be there because of the state of emergency.

Accra is quite a city. Cleaner and more cared for than Lagos with impressive government buildings. A guard tried to stop us from taking pictures of them but we teased them and finally did. I hope they come out.

The next day we took a plane with Ghana Airways to Abidjan. We spent ten days in Abidjan, which was restful and wonderful practice for my French. Abidjan is incredibly expensive and we worried constantly about money. We stayed at Hôtel International for five days, which was the least expensive—1,600 francs for a non-air-conditioned room, but it was an 80-franc taxi ride from town. We got about 686 francs to the British pound (traveler's cheques) and only 570 to the Nigerian pound. We got to know some English "limeys"

PEACE CORPS

WASHINGTON

OFFICE OF
THE DIRECTOR

December 14, 1962

Dear Dorothy,

In recent months I have had the opportunity to visit Peace Corps Volunteers at work in 10 different nations. Nearly everything I have seen has caused my admiration to grow. The spirit, motivation and competence of the Volunteers impresses everyone, but most of all it is their spirit.

In my judgment, this spirit is the true spirit of Christmas because it embodies, in many, many cases, the true giving of self without solely selfish reasons. It is this spirit that promises the lasting peace which has so long eluded the grasp of mankind.

For your contribution to this important work around the world, I thank you, and in doing so, offer you every good wish for a new year filled with success and happiness.

Merry Christmas and a Happy New Year.

Sincerely,

Sargent Shriver

and spent a day on a cruise on their oil tanker with several French people—very pleasant.

Then we moved out to Grand-Bassam for two days. It used to be the capital before the war. A quiet town, the only noise the pounding surf.

We came back into Abidjan and wandered into the new Peace Corps headquarters where we met two volunteers from Nigeria we had anticipated meeting. They were flying on to Sierra Leone and Liberia. In Abidjan we met an interesting young couple on a travel study grant to French West Africa, who had already lived a year in Dakar. We discussed the differences between French and British Africa. The French have never felt any paternal responsibility for the Africans. They treat the African as they would anyone else—a kind of laissez-faire approach. Everyone is on their own.

The French do teach in the schools but thousands and thousands of them (the majority) come to make money—enough to return to France comfortably. Meanwhile, the French make Africa their home, children go to African schools, the grandparents live with them. One sees all ages—particularly it struck me to see groups of teenagers. The British send their children to school in London or Switzerland—they visit on Christmas holidays. One never sees teenagers somehow.

The most striking thing about French West Africa though is to see *all* of the shops run by French, occasionally with African helpers. In all of Ghana and Nigeria there are *no* shops run by Britishers. France pours millions of francs into Africa, but one can imagine the millions taken out—Everything is imported, from fancy oranges to yards of velvet, glassware, wine, mineral water—the French bring their whole way of life. The shops are exquisite—air conditioned, clean, beautifully decorated—they could have easily been in Paris.

The cities in French West Africa are clean, beautifully landscaped, modern—one could easily imagine oneself in a European city in Abidjan. The French have set an example for the Africans here, which I think the British failed to do. Cities in British West Africa are often dirty, with vendors all over the streets. Open sewers, some six feet across, narrow unpaved streets, and the stores not particularly attractive. The banks, embassies, and some office buildings are the most attractive buildings in Lagos. More significant than appearance, however, are the French people themselves. Whereas the British have sent their best people to govern the colonies, the class of Frenchmen one finds in Africa must be the worst—insensitive, money-conscious, and used to dirty conditions. They don't filter or boil the water, or use any disinfectant on fresh vegetables, for instance.

The British person may not be an academic person, but usually knows something about Africa. The French often do not. They are thoroughly provincial. They pay no attention to anyone but their little colony. This makes things particularly tough for the PCVs there for instance. Almost all of the group (thirty-one) are stationed by themselves. The only other expatriates being the French. Often the French have not invited them over or displayed any curiosity about who they are. If they show any evidence of having African friends— the French would have nothing to do with them.

Love,
Dot

*Kwame Nkrumah was the first president and prime minister of Ghana.

Letter from Hershel of January 14, 1963

Dear Mrs. Crews,

Dottie and I had a wonderful trip to the Ivory Coast and found Abidjan quite a change from cities that we've seen in Nigeria. Abidjan is very European at its center though African at the fringes and in the hinterland. A Parisian atmosphere pervades the town center called "le Plateau," which has street cafés, specialty shops of various sorts, beautifully landscaped parks, and marvelous restaurants.

Our voyage back to Lagos was fun and restful. We were never really very far from land as the "boat followed the coastline and we stopped in Takoradi, Lomé, and Cotonou before arriving in

Lagos. Well, after all this vacationing Dottie and I are ready to go back to our classrooms and students.

You ask when Dottie and I are returning to the U.S. Dottie finishes her university teaching in June and I finish my second term in late July. As soon as I'm finished we plan to take off for the States via various cities in the Mediterranean and Europe. We'll be back to New York in mid-August. My plans are to begin law school in September 1963.

I sent away applications, transcripts, letters of recommendation, etc. to NYU and Hastings College of Law. The next big item on my agenda is the Law School Entrance Examination, which I will take on February 9. I probably will not know if I have been accepted until April.

The dean of the School of Law at the University of California sent me a copy of a letter which he sent to NYU, Hastings, and Columbia after I had informed him of my application to those schools.

"Gentlemen:

Mr. Hershel Zelig Herzberg entered the School of law, University of California, Berkeley, in September of 1956 and attended until February 4, 1957 at which time he withdrew and was given an honorable dismissal. He was eligible to continue at the time."

This letter will be of some help when the schools are considering my application.

Mr. Crews's plywood case really sounds exciting. Please send us some clippings about the case.

All of the packages that you sent have arrived safely. Many thanks for the Spanish records. Best regards to Mr. Crews.

Sincerely,

Hershel

Letter of January 15, 1963

… Incidentally, I am reminded of this last visit of assorted PCVs. Two of my UCLA group set off for East Africa by lorry, bus, taxi, or anyway they could get there. One had his mother working in the YMCA in Uganda and wanted to see her. Somehow they didn't get there when she expected them and she contacted the American Embassy, which sent out a search. They found them probably in some village waiting for a truck, which only comes through once a week or something, and flew them to Uganda.

Then another PCV from Sierra Leone went out fishing with two Catholic fathers (one his headmaster) and an African in the Gulf of Guinea. The undertow is very bad and they were soon swept out. A wave caught the boat the wrong way and they capsized. They couldn't right the boat so clung to it. One of the fathers couldn't swim and kept passing out. The African panicked and eventually those two drowned. The Catholic father (headmaster) and the PCV clung to the craft while the sharks circled, and eventually righted it. They tore off the floorboards to steady it and drifted sixty-six hours in the sun and cold nights. Finally a plane spotted them off the coast of Monrovia and they are in a hospital now. Whew!…

Anyway, we left Abidjan December 31 at about 8:30 p.m. in a *big* passenger/cargo boat of the Frassinet line. The French cooking was delicious. The boat had come from Marseilles and was going to the Congo. Passengers included the bishop of Douala who was returning from the Ecumenical Council in Rome, several assorted monks who all drank and smoked, assorted French, Germans, Africans, and a most attractive American Negro couple who were working on an Encyclopedia Africana in Dahomey. It will include all of Africa …

Letter of January 25, 1963

... We have had some interesting dinner parties lately—figured out we have had about twenty guests this month, which is hard on the budget. Besides members of the language department—includes a new acquisition of a Scotchman to teach French. The latter has just arrived and is a bit too rigid and provincial to be popular here. We had a big party with the Irish faculty including a new couple, a very charming Nigerian married to a little Irish girl. They have been gulped up by the university and seem to be involved in everything. He teaches African literature and his father is a minister. He was a former student of Father Butler's and some of the other fathers around here. He is Donatus Nwaga and will one day be quite well-known I predict. Then also we invited the university registrar and his wife. He is a very fine American Negro. His daughter went to the university here last year; now she is at Howard. He has been right in the midst of all of the tensions and turmoil and hasn't really gotten to know much of Africa ...

January 1963 to August 1963

The last eight months went very fast. At the university, the students were screened and reenrolled, and classes resumed. Students enjoyed learning French and you could hear *bonjour* and *au revoir* all over campus.

Chicken projects that other Peace Corps volunteers were developing in surrounding villages were producing eggs. Villagers were learning how to manage raising chickens carefully with steady feeding instead of just letting them run wild in the bush. Nigerians loved curry chicken and considered it a national dish even though curry had been introduced by the English.

Back in the States, the Civil Rights Movement was heating up. It was difficult to explain front-page photos of demonstrations with dogs and water being used against the protesters. The university administrators—the chancellor, registrar, and others—were African-Americans from Michigan State. There was a social distance between them and Nigerians. Nigerians would say proudly that they were never slaves. They felt a certain contempt even though obviously the African-Americans living amongst them were never slaves.

Over the years many of my African-American friends and colleagues have asked me what would it be like if they went to Africa. Some are afraid to go. Would they be treated with scorn? This is hard to assess. Many Nigerians want to come to America and understand the value of having contacts, so they would be eager to meet them. In the bush there is probably not much information. They would be treated with curiosity as we were.

I always felt welcome and safe. In the villages, children would swarm around me, often trying to touch me. White women were not often seen. Africa is mostly a male-dominated society, but they accepted me as a teacher, visitor, or someone coming to help them.

It is easy to be lethargic in the intense heat of the tropics. I found it very important to keep busy even though staying indoors, drinking cold beverages, and being quiet often seemed preferable.

Dorothy in her office in the French Department

Toys from America
Well-Baby Clinic

An American athlete, Mel Whitfield, arranged for an organization in Los Angeles to send hundreds of toys. Nigerian children in the bush had no toys. They played with sticks, stones, and natural objects. Animals were all around them in the bush, but not to play with. Bright, colorful plastic toys were a fascination, especially Mickey Mouse watches.

The health center arranged for a well-baby clinic and hundreds of mothers came with their babies. Some of us were judges. We looked carefully over the babies. Elizabeth Leedam, the WHO person, and nurses helped us. It is extremely difficult to raise children in the tropical rain forest. All tiny bacteria grows out of control. If you scratched yourself, within half an hour it would look red and angry, and could become infected easily. Mothers had no access to any ointments or other medication for fevers for example, which were common and usually meant malaria. In the bush, no one took quinine. We took chloroquine (quinine) tablets every week to protect us.

Babies could have fevers, rashes, worms, schistosomiasis, filariasis, or malnourishment. There was little access to protein or fruit, or understanding of a balanced diet.

So, we were delighted to award well babies. The mothers were very proud and pleased. Babies are nursed for about nine months and then put on the ground and eat anything. Children were vulnerable to everything from unsafe water to mosquitoes. It seemed almost miraculous they survived to become toddlers.

People had noticed that expatriates often referred to some object on their wrists and time seemed very important to them. So Mickey Mouse watches were treasured. The colors and textures of the toys were a fascination.

Toys from America

Well-baby clinic

```
                                                    1st Feb. 1963.

Event    :  Baby Contest.
Place    :  OVAKO, Eastern Region.
Purpose  :  To Stimulate proper interest in the growth and development
            of the child in an indigenous setting.
Content  :  The aspect which we are most interested in today, is
            "Infant Welfare", As all these babies here, regularly attend
            the Clinics held at those Health Centers.
            Ages arranging from 6 months to 1 year and over.

                The Health Centers are primarly concerned with all
            enviormental aspects of the child and parent.

                This Health Center at OVAKO, is typical of those being
            developed throughout Eastern Region, giving assistance
            by the (W.H.O.) World Health Organization.

Participants: The babies here today, are from Nsukka, Ibagwa, Opi,
            Isi - Enu, Obono - Afor, Enugu Ezike, etc. These Health
            Centers are located throughout the northern section of the
            Eastern Region.

                Judges: Persons who are acting as judges are as
            follows:
                    1.  Miss Elizabeth Leedam, Head, Training Nurse
                        from (W.H.O.) Miss Leedam, is primarly concern
                        in developing, nutritional and child health
                        services in Eastern Region. Presently, Miss.
                        Leedam, is assigned to the Eastern Region
                        Government for the past (2) years, her duties
                        have been principly in the Nsukka area.
                    2.  Mrs. _____ Ike, wife of the Assistant Registrar
                                            UNN.
                    3.  Mrs. Louella Morton, wife of the Registrar UNN.
                    4.  Mrs. Dorothy Hergberg, U.S. Peace Corps and
                                            Lecturer.
                    5.  Mrs. L. B. Perry, wife of the Dean of Student Affairs
                                            UNN.
                    6.  Mrs. Helen Bratcher, Lecturer, Home Economics
                                            UNN.
                    7.  Sister _____ from St. Teresa's Hospital
                    8.  Mrs. _____
                    9.  Mrs. _____ Smith, wife of U.S. Consulate,
                                            Enugu. (E.R.)
```

Original documents for the baby contest and show

Prizes: A Toy will be awarded the child whose parents has kept with the set standards in Personal hygienes, introduced by the Health Centers' Assistances found in each Clinic. No Child can compete if his parents have not stuck to the hard fast health standards.

Donators of Toys are Mr. and Mrs. Alvin Greene and the Civic Minded Citizens of Los Angeles, California, U.S.A.

This Toy Project was founded by Mr. Mal Whitfield, three years ago when he was assigned in Liberia, West Africa.

The idea was to assist in forthering "Goodwill" among African and American alike.

Transportation: The Transporting of these toys from Los Angeles, California to Nigeria, was arranged through the Presidents People-To-People Sports Committee, Inc.; The U.S. Ambassador, Mr. Joseph Palmer, 11; Lt. General, Joe Kelly, Commander Military Air Transportation Services, United States Air Force; Col. Robert J. Sunde, Commander, 1611th Base Group, McGuire Air Force Base; Mr. James Ferrel, President Ferrel Lines and Mr. Leon Santini of (7) Brothers Moving Van Company, N.Y.

1st February, 1963.

PROGRAMME FOR BABY SHOW:

1. Welcome address by Dr. Ozoh.
2. Selection of prize-winners by Judges.
3. Distribution of prizes by age groups.

    0 - 6 Months   1st, 2nd, 3rd.
    6 - 1 Year   1st, 2nd, 3rd.
    1 - 1½ Years.   1st, 2nd, 3rd.

    Consolation prizes:-

    Twins.

    Motherless.

    Regular Clinic attendants-Mothers.

4. Vote of thanks by Mrs. I. N. Ugwuh, Senior Health Sister.
5. Response by Mr. Mal-Whitefield.
6. Light Refreshment.

Letter of February 1, 1963

… Yesterday Father McGlade had the opening of his borehole with the new African bishop of Enugu, Bishop Anyogu, blessing it. The ministers of local government were there, the Honorable John Nwodo and P.N. Okei. Also members of the Peace Corps, the press, and some of the university community were there. There were two boreholes to be blessed. We went to the biggest one at about 4:00 p.m. The crowd and the bishop went to the smallest one first, so we waited in the hot sun for about an hour and a half. Finally they came.

The people were so excited. There was dancing, palm wine, drums, and dengue guns. Father is constructing another church just like his other one. The big skeleton of that hovered one hundred feet from the borehole. Interesting psychology, *n'est-ce pas?* In the course of the day Father was presented with cows, goats, and about a hundred eggs. The eggs were very precious to the villagers. But these were rotten and smelled. Both places were christened "Father McGlade's Borehole." The bishop was most personable and it was altogether a most colorful day.

Then today I was invited to be one of the judges of a baby show. Mel Whitfield, an Olympic gold medalist for the U.S. who has been coaching athletics in Africa for four years, arranged to have three thousand toys and pounds of clothes sent from Los Angeles. Some of these were distributed to the Home Economics Department of the university for demonstration, some to a couple of schools, some to a maternity program of the health center, and today about a hundred toys as prizes in a well-baby show. The best (healthiest) babies from outlying clinics were selected and told to come. They came and sat silently from 8:00 a.m. until we arrived. Altogether there were ten judges. There were sisters from the hospital. They had already received some toys for an orphanage they run. There were Nigerians from the university. Elizabeth the WHO nurse from the health center was there too.

We selected those babies without umbilical hernias, scabies, rashes, and with vaccination marks, if over three months. We also looked for undernourishment. We were really rewarding the mothers for having healthy babies. The best toys were given to the winners, but everyone got something. It went beautifully. They especially loved the plastic Mickey Mouse watches, tops, and little tea sets ...

Father McGlade in front of the water tank receiving gifts

One of the winners of the baby contest

Letter from Hershel of February 19, 1963

Dear Mr. and Mrs. Crews,

The school term is in full swing. Both Dottie and I are fully engrossed in a variety of activities in addition to our teaching. Dottie has some good sewing projects close to Nsukka to work on now. Before, she had been driving fifteen to twenty miles to the bush to run her sewing projects. This term she has developed some projects in the immediate Nsukka area, which saves her a lot of travel. The girls here need as much help as those girls twenty miles away.

Dottie has begun teaching a junior staff class at the university two days per week, in addition to her regular twelve classes. She has many more papers to correct now.

I'm still working with my afternoon German class four days per week. This term I'm conducting two special afternoon history classes to help boys who were in 4A last year who now find themselves in 5B History after having missed one year of history class last year. These boys need filling in on a year's work in history because they plan to take the history examination paper in the West African School Certificate Examination at the end of fifth year. Coaching athletics and running my sickroom complete my daily schedule. What with corrections of weekly English essays and exercises as well as history exercises and examinations, I keep busy. My Igbo work is slowing down, but I am still progressing.

Last week I read for the part of Max in the play Dial M for Murder by Frederick Knott, which is being put on by some of the lecturers at the university. The play will be put on in about three weeks and should be a lot of fun.

Both Dot and I agree with your decision not to come to Nigeria because of scheduling and health difficulties. We'll be seeing you this summer in the U.S. As I've written you, Dottie and I will be leaving Nigeria in late July or early August to return to the States after about a month of traveling in Europe, so that I can begin law school in September.

I took the Law School Entrance Exam on February 9 at the University of Nigeria. It will probably take a few weeks to a month before I get the results, let alone hear from the law schools to which I have applied. The test was the IBM type, which should be scored fairly fast.

The weather here is dry and cool except for midday, which lasts from 11:00 a.m. till 5:00 p.m. when it is very hot. All in all Nsukka is quite pleasant and comfortable. A few weeks ago we were having some water difficulties because the water pumps were overburdened by Nsukka's vast consumption of water. Since then new pumps have been added so our water supply is back to normal.

My birthday was really made memorable by the gift Dottie gave me. It was an Agfa Silette 35mm camera. This camera will give us some larger slides than Dottie's small Japanese camera.

The Louisville trial sounds, from all your accounts, interesting. It must be pretty exasperating when you realize the opposition is protracting the trial as long as possible

It's really a shame to see the great newspapers of New York shut down for so long. Both the unions and management seem to be doing everything possible to stimulate Congress to enact laws, which will require compulsory government-supervised arbitration. Many of the union men don't seem to realize that they may be killing a good number of the New York papers and that they may lose their jobs if some papers fold. That is what happened to the Brooklyn Eagle some years ago.

Well, I've got to sign off for now. Hope to hear from you soon.
Sincerely,
Hersh

Letter of February 19, 1963

… I have a new French class with the junior staff of the university. These are secretaries, clerks, accountants from each department. The Peace Corps at the university started this program for them. Mostly there are English, history, and math classes. This program is entirely the brainchild of the Peace Corps.

Some of the wives of lecturers have helped out too. It is sort of a new thing in British Africa to speak French. Some one hundred people have turned up for the class!!! I have given a test, much homework, spoken French, and gone quickly through the book to see who is serious. At least forty stayed with it. Only nineteen have submitted homework so I hope eventually it will come down to a reasonable size. Both the clerks in the Language Department come to the class.

People say there isn't an office on campus that you walk into now that you don't hear *Bonjour!!!*…

Letter of February 24, 1963

Dear Folks,

I had thought I had written you about once a week at least so I'm surprised at your saying you haven't received a letter for some time. I am enjoying the end of a lovely four-day weekend at the end of Ramadan. Most stores and the university were closed. I have spent it reading, sleeping, and sewing. I seem to have gotten very tired and I feel much better now. I have just finished two rather wild sack dresses—now I have to find the courage to wear them. One was made from material given me by the Russian family—glazed black-and-white cotton print; the other was something like "native" cloth. Altogether I've made seven dresses, two blouses, and two skirts for myself over the last year. Also I've given some away and some of the clothes I brought with me. I've only bought three dresses and a few other items. On the whole, my wardrobe has held up. By the time the dust is scrubbed out with cold water and soap, things turn to rags overnight.

Happy Birthday, Daddy!!! It's because it comes so near after Christmas, one forgets that anyone could have a birthday so near Christmas! So it is a month and three days since your sixty-third birthday, Pop. Congratulations!! Hersh has a birthday on February 4.

I'm glad about your decision not to come to Africa. Some of the parents of PCVs have actually come for a visit. Frankly, I think you would be uncomfortable. The exciting part about Africa is watching it grow and change and develop—which one must live here and work here to appreciate. Just a quick visit is most misleading.... I will be anxious to reread my first impressions of Africa.... How confused I now imagine they must be!

Our five kittens are thriving—now four weeks old. They look like wound up little toys running about the room. I had someone show Isaiah how to bake bread. So he bakes it about three times a week now and it smells delicious when it is baking—I just took a fresh loaf out of the oven. The market bread is hard and rubbery by comparison. Yesterday I experimented with some canned powdery substance and milk and made strawberry ice cream! It wasn't bad.

Love,
Dot

Letter of March 3, 1963

... This week has been full of episodes.

Through the efforts of a young German who teaches at the College of Languages, a German classical guitarist came to give a concert at Nsukka. Professor Siegfried Behrend arrived. One of the students introduced him with some very blunt statements to the students:

"You are going to hear the guitar played tonight as you have never heard it before. I am sure that if you give it a chance you will enjoy it. Professor Behrend tells me that when he played at the University of Dakar half the audience walked out after the first piece. I have assured him that that will not happen here!"

Behrend played quite a nice arrangement of "Greensleeves." Halfway through there was a banging on the doors and he stopped. About twenty people were waiting to come in, among them Chukudebe, Zik's representative on campus. And a graduate of Oxford. This was the first embarrassment.

He finished "Greensleeves." He was playing an English country dance. Murmurings got louder and louder. Looking up I saw the students snaking down the aisle. Finally the noise got too loud to ignore. The lights were turned on and he was taken off the stage. About two hundred students left. The faculty of about a hundred sat frozen in incredulity that they could really be leaving. Behrend came back on stage. We gave him a standing ovation and he played the rest of the concert.

Some of the publicity of him I saw called him better than Segovia because his repertoire was larger and technique flawless. He is in his thirties and has traveled all over the world. There were editorials in the Nsukka paper this morning. Everyone is still stunned. Many of the students have agreed that it was rather "bush" behavior. We saw the guitarist at a party after the concert and he was not upset. We talked about the African's musical talent being mostly rhythmical. They find something lyrical without a strong rhythm hard to learn and difficult to comprehend. The university chorus that tries to sing the *Messiah* was ghastly …

Letter of March 8, 1963

Dear Folks,

Jill died at 1:00 a.m., March 6.

She regained consciousness Friday when her husband came home from Sweden and was even talking. Then suddenly late Wednesday night she began to have trouble breathing. For some reason the doctor was not called immediately—not till 1:00 a.m. when it was too late.

The illness and funeral were a nightmare indescribable. She had had her appendix out and seemed to be recovering fine but suddenly collapsed and they operated again. They found she had a colitis-infected intestinal tract. Where or why this developed no one knows. One can't help thinking that the surgery might not have been carefully done. The wound seemed to be draining well although she was unconscious and with a high fever for a week. If her general physical condition had been better, she would have had a better chance. Then Wednesday night, Eyo, her husband, thought of just dropping by to see her again. When she first had difficulty breathing, the doctor should have been notified. Again this would never have happened had she been under English or American supervision.

We drove into Enugu for services and after that a long slow funeral procession of a hundred cars—the minister of education himself came. When we got to the cemetery the grave was not dug. We stood in complete silence—about two hundred people—while the workers argued and worked, and figured it out. It was an absolute nightmare. By the time it was finished, people were hysterical. All of Queens School were there wailing unearthly.

Which makes me all the more relieved that you are not coming to Africa and that I will be leaving.

Love,
Dot

Letter of March 14, 1963

... We had a meeting of just the French Department. How fast this year has gone! We discussed final exams and I am to set the exam for the first year minors, which includes some two hundred students. Minors means that they are taking French to fulfill a requirement. They are not majoring in French. I have three classes of them, which is about ninety students ...

Letter from Hershel of March 15, 1963

Deer Mr. and Mrs. Crews,

Dottie has written you about my decision to attend Hastings College in San Francisco. We shall leave Nsukka about the 30th of July and begin our grand tour home. We hope to be in New York by the 23rd of August. We'll spend over a week in New York and then head for San Francisco by the day after Labor Day. I want to get settled and organized by September 9 when registration gets under way.

This term seems to have flown by and it's hard to believe that examinations will begin in two weeks. Dottie and I are not making any long trips during this vacation because Dottie has no vacation really and I want to finish my Igbo phrase book. During the vacation I'll be working on a cataloging project in the university library and working on Igbo in the afternoons and evenings.

The St. Teresa College Magazine came out last Friday and was nearly a complete sellout at 4 pence a copy. I'll send you a copy because I think it gives the flavor of the STC campus. I'm sure you'll find it exotic and amusing.

Yesterday two of the junior staff tutors who are in my German class invited me to visit their village about twenty miles from Nsukka. It was really an amazing and moving experience for me. These chaps come from very humble homes where they are the only children in their respective families to have received a high school education. The entire village came out to see. Me, and my mere presence provided a Sunday afternoon's entertainment. Some thanked me profusely for visiting their underdeveloped village and begged me to make comments on how they could improve their condition and achieve a higher standard. After touring their mud and thatch huts, and a local fetish juju shrine, I was seated at a table in the chief's house and given fresh undiluted palm wine. We exchanged many toasts and I was presented with eight bottles of Guinness Stout, five bottles of Orange Drink, three bottles of Pepsi, a rooster, and about a dozen eggs. If you could have seen the people and their condition I believe that you would understand how overwhelmed I was by their generosity; in this village a man who lives on 10 shillings ($1.40) a month is thought to be doing very well, and most live on much less. Each bottle of stout alone cost at least 2 shillings, so this gives you some idea of their bounty. They absolutely insisted on my taking the gifts, and so I finally accepted though reluctantly. Most of the villagers have never seen a white woman and when they were told I had a wife, they insisted that I bring her on the next visit I make to their village. From what I gathered if I could only give them advance notice, next time thousands would turn out to see Dottie. Oh, by the way, the Igbo that I know came in handy and made everybody quite happy.

 Sincerely,

 Hershel

Letter of April 4, 1963

Dear Folks,

My Style Show was this afternoon. There were twenty-nine dresses in all and five judges. The judges deliberated long and slowly, and finally came to a decision. There were twelve prizes and twenty toothbrushes for the rest.

I bought three prizes. A couple of others were donated and the rest were large remnants of material, each big enough for a blouse—some mine and some given to me by other people who went home. I think the girls enjoyed the show and the prizes. It was the first fashion show in Nsukka and I'm sure they had no idea what it was going to be like. But when they came out and walked before the judges, they were surprisingly poised. About ten to fifteen people came from the university—the whole Home Economics Department was impressed.

Anyway, it was fun and I hope it gave the girls a sense of pride in having sewn something themselves. Sewing is only beginning to be appreciated, instead of a piece of cloth just wrapped around themselves in the villages. In school the girls have uniforms of course.

The Peace Corps contingent from the university arrived late but took some photos.

Love,
Dot

Participants at the Style Show

ANNOUNCER GREETS ALL
STYLE SHOW AT QUEEN OF THE ROSARY SCHOOL, NSUKKA, NIGERIA
APRIL 4, 1963

1. Lelia Ude. Lelia has made a checked dress with a round neck and bow in back.
2. Eunice Okoye. Eunice has made a sun-back dress in blue with a side opening.
3. Edna Oti. Edna has chosen a material of yellow flowers for her dress. She has added a bow in the front as well as the back.
4. Virginia Edoga. Virginia has made a round-necked dress of white material with blue stars.
5. Mary Rose Ezemenari. Mary's dress is all yellow with a square neckline in the back and a bow.
6. Dorothy Bepeh. Dorothy's dress is of flowered material with a round neck. She has a side zipper and buttons as well.
7. Matnzeen Ilozaomha. Maureen's dress has a square neckline in the front and round neckline in back.
8. Beatrice Eneh. Beatrice has made a dress of blue-patterned material with a V neck and a low back.
9. Francisca Thompson. Francisca has made a yellow dress with a V neck.
10. Monica Ihekwe. Monica has made a sun-backed checked dress. She has added a special green sash.
11. Lilian Ukaeghu. Lilian's dress is all green with a round neckline in front and square neckline in back.
12. Philomena Ezeadum. Philomena's dress is in the sun-back style of blue material She has added a sash.
13. Christine Eleamu. Christine's "brown andorange-patterned dress has a square neckline in front and she has added a wide belt.
14. Winifred Ononye. Winifred's dress is all pink with a square neckline in back.

15. Fidelia Akan. Fidelia's dress of yellow flowers has a round neckline.
16. Caroline Ekekezie. Caroline's dress is blue with a round neckline in back and front.
17. Catherine Ezimorah. Cathoine's dress of blue flowers is in the sun-back style.
18. Priscilia Tjmeamo. Priscilla's dress of yellow flowers is completed by a bow in the back.
19. Caroline Anekwe. Caroline has made a dress of orange and brown-patterned material with a square neckline.
20. Rebecca Eze. Rebecca has made a dress of blue-flowered material with a round neck and square neckline in the back.
22. Francisca Ukuta. Francisca's green sun-back dress has white straps added.
23. Maria Chinewu. Maria has made a dress of blue material with a square neckline in front and round in back.
24. Teresa Nwachio. Teresa's material of blue diamonds has been styled into a dress with a round neckline.
25. Victoria Epundu. Victoria has made a blue dress in the sun-back style.
26. Virginia Amah. Virginia's dress is brown and orange with a V neckline in front and a V neckline in back.
27. Cecelia Enumuo. In a material of yellow flowers, Cecilia's dress has a square neckline in front.
28. Felicia Onyeri. Felicia's dress is blue-patterned material in the sun-back style.
29. Josephine Ezeapo. Josephine's dress of orange and brown has a square neckline in front with a round back.
30. Maria Okofor. Due to some difficulties, Maria just began her dress this week. She has made a white bodice with a skirt of starred material.

Style Show, Queen of the Rosary School, April 4, 1963
Note to the judges

It is possible that numbers 21, Mary Mbah, and 24, Teresa Nwachie will not enter. Their dresses are short. Please give Mary Mbah, Teresa Nwachie, and Mercy Okonkwo toothbrushes at the end, however. The girls will come once through singly and then in pairs, and then all together. If you wish to see any of them again, please ask. You may decide on any method of judging—possibly a point system, although not necessarily. Perhaps you could announce the points, the details you were looking for.

Prizes: The prizes are numbered just to provide some sort of guide. I would suggest there be only one first prize and only one second. There could be a tie for third, and so forth.

The girls have added some touches to their dress—such as bows and white sashes, which do not appear in the commentary.

126 **Me, Madam**

Audience and participants at the Style Show

Letter of April 10, 1963

Dear Folks,

We are beginning a four-day weekend tomorrow and we plan to go with a Nigerian friend down south again to the market at Ikot Ekpene. We will buy some more curios, the last we probably will get. Hersh has finished exams and classes, so is on vacation until the middle of May. The university still has classes straight through without a stop until May 31. It is really a wild schedule to have eighteen weeks of classes, but that is how the committee of the faculty scheduled it after the riots last October—to get the same number of weeks in before graduation.

We have recently been told that the students who are graduating will stop classes a few weeks before the others in order to study for their comprehensive exams in their majors. This is rather bizarre and means they will have separate final exams! I guess they are nervous about their first graduates. Already all the roads Zik will use are being landscaped, parking lots made, signposts repaired.

The acting head of the Nigerian project is in Washington now and has won a case. We were notified that any termination of the first UCLA project (me) or Harvard project (Hersh) before December 1963 would not be considered for compelling reasons, but accepted for normal completion of tour of duty. This is very reasonable as we really have completed our contracts. Even if I did stay until September, the university doesn't open until October. St Teresa's opens late in September.

This week we went to a ceremony in one of the villages about a Young Farmers Club and chicken house that one of the Peace Corps has been setting up—I think he has five such projects going in this particular village. The Young Farmers built the chicken houses and then three-hundred-day-old baby chicks were supplied by the minister of agriculture. About thirty died of pneumonia. They raised the rest and have recently sold the big fat cocks—150 of them—for about 50 pounds in total ($150), which paid all their feed bills and costs so far, and some left over. Soon within the next month or so the hens will start laying, which means profit. They plan to sell to the university and two other villages. One of the agricultural students at the university is in charge of the project under the PCV's supervision. The PCV is due to go home but he is trying to contract with AID for he and his wife to stay another year. The Young Farmers want to start piggeries next. In each village where he has chickens, the chicken house is the center of village activity! Quite impressive!

Recently I have been doing some typing for the university—the entrance examinations which are being given in May. Each department submits an exam, in addition to a long general knowledge exam. I have done twenty-two stencils in six hours of work at night!

Love,
Dot

Letter of April 15, 1963

Dear Folks,

We have just come back from a lovely relaxing trip over the four-day Easter weekend—to Umuahia, Ikot Ekpene, and Aba—with a Nigerian friend of ours, actually the assistant registrar at the university whom I have come to know through some problems concerning the graduating students. He is a very nice guy with a British wife—actually Welsh—they met at the University of Wales. He has been at the university since its beginning, being trained to be one of the permanent staff. Their name is Usoro. They knew Jill, as they lived in Enugu at one time. He knew Jill's husband.

Hersh learned today the results of the West African School Certificate Exam, which all secondary school curriculums in West Africa are set for. The kids study for the exam for five years. The results are tabulated in Ibadan now, formerly in England. Hersh was the only member of the staff of St. Teresa's who had no one flunk!!! Even boys who flunked everything else! The boys are thrilled and will now listen to him worshipfully in class of course!

The fathers are pleased. That really is very good. He stenciled about fifty pages of notes for the boys to study outside of their texts—these stencils will be left for boys in later years. St. Teresa's results were very good this year and they just might get permission for high school classes from the minister this year.

Something else important happens—tomorrow!

Happy Birthday to you ... Happy Birthday, dear mother. There really isn't anything I can buy for you here but we are sending boxes of curios home and you can pick out something.

On our trip we saw some of the palm oil factories, which the Eastern Nigerian Development Commission is developing to exploit the palm oil products. The palm kernel, big and red, is crushed and the oil pours out boiling hot from the machines. It is bottled and sold to other countries in the Commonwealth. It is used for cooking—we have palm oil sauce and rice or yam every day for lunch. We saw a huge beer factory which a Dutch firm is building—with a bottling plant built by the East Nigerian Development Commission next to it. There is one brand (Star Lager) made in Nigeria, and other brands imported. The hops and other ingredients grow in Nigeria and it is one industry that could be quickly profitable here.

Some skill crafts shops—such as Okigwe pottery and Awka wood carving are being sponsored by the Eastern Nigerian Development Commission to keep the craftsmen going; the skills had been dying out. At Aba we saw a film about [boxer] Dick Tiger; actually his hometown was Aba. And the film, made in America, showed this. The audience went wild. He is really admired. A newsreel we saw had the Eichman trial. Another had the 1961 census In Britain.

Love,
Dot

Letter of April 19, 1963

Dear Folks,

This week has been so busy with guests and people visiting that it seems never to end. Vanchee has come back! He is the Indian friend who lives next door who has been on leave in India since December. He wanted very much to be married and talked last year of nothing else. For three months at home he interviewed applicants. You know, their horoscopes have to match. He had given up hope of finding anyone. She had to be Brahman and as he is quite brilliant, he wanted an educated girl. Then with two weeks left, he met the girl on a Sunday, married her the next Sunday, and the next Sunday arrived in Nigeria!

She is quite tiny—he is very small too. She has a BA Honors in history, sings, dances, and plays a complicated stringed instrument called a *veena*. She is only twenty-three but full of life! They are just perfect for each other; the horoscope system must be good! He has been transferred to Afikpo and everyone is very sorry about this. They are rushing around visiting people. We looked over their wedding gifts and have had some chance to visit with them.

Then Hersh's friend from Ibadan—a student he knew there—has been here all week on visit. Then we had people over for dinner and bridge. It always requires two hours to prepare a meal, even with both of us working at it.

Four PCVs arrived from the bush this week to brush up their French. They have been around the department listening to records, attending classes, and talking to us.

Last night we went to a performance of *King Kong*—South African operetta—performed by students. Each year the Music Department,—which is largely the achievement of a large Negro woman with a PhD in music and quite talented—presets a production. Last year it was *Aida,* with some help from the faculty in singing. This year it was a completely student production. It was surprisingly good considering that none of the cast had ever done anything like it before. The dances were the best!

You wrote something about a reunion the end of August or early September in San Francisco. I think the idea is wonderful except for the timing. We hope to leave Nigeria by August 5, travel to Israel, East Europe, Germany, and England—which is not only a grand tour but also a chance to relax—and reach the States sometime in August. We want to spend as much time as possible in New York, then fly out to California. Hersh begins classes September 9. But during September we must find a place to live, buy a car, buy clothes, household furnishings. I must find a job. In short there couldn't possibly be a worse time for us to cope with a reunion. I wrote to Mac and suggested Christmas as a possible time for it.

Love,
Dot

Letter of May 3, 1963

... We have made new friends—the Usoros. He is the assistant registrar of the university. He asked Hersh to help put all the papers together and package them, etc. (for the entrance exams). Hersh has been working in his office every day for two weeks. It has been perfect, as St. Teresa's is on holidays and the fathers have the car. So every morning Mr. Usoro picks us up. I don't know what we would have done otherwise. We have been shopping in a taxi once or twice even so. Without a car, life is very difficult here. When the gas cylinder goes off, one can't cook anything until it is replaced, for example.

Many of the American faculty and all of the Peace Corps are leaving in six to eight weeks. It will be awful when they leave, but the thought that we will be leaving as well makes it bearable. We have our ticket. We had to reserve them early in order to take advantage of the half-rate airline rates. They go up this month. There were special rates for transit travel, which means spending one night here, two there, etc. But now one has to pay full fare.

We will fly from Enugu to Lagos on July 27. We have our final medical exams on July 30, 31, and fly to Cairo on August 1. Hersh has the suspicion that King Hussein in Jordan will lose his throne about that time. He thinks that the entire Arab Alliance will march on Israel, which will make a state of emergency throughout the Middle East. In which case we won't get off. But on to Rome!

Love,
Dot

Letter from Hershel of May 5, 1963

Dear Mr. and Mrs. Crews,

Since April 15 I've been working at the university helping the assistant registrar with the entrance examinations as my vacation project. Both Dottie and I are going to be invigilators for the exam, which will be given next week. Dottie is going to Benin and I'm going to Ibadan. These are the same exams that Dottie typed.

We have arranged for our flight home with KLM. We were fortunate to be able to take advantage of the "extra cities for no extra fare" offer, which the international airlines abolished last month because they were losing too much money. We'll leave Enugu on the 27th of July for Lagos where we will spend about three days taking medical examinations and getting processed out of the Peace Corps. On August 1 we leave for Cairo and then it's back to the U.S. via Cyprus, Israel, Athens, Vienna, Munich, Amsterdam, and London. We'll arrive in New York on the 20th of August.

School resumes here on the 15th of May and I'm looking forward to returning to the classroom.

My Igbo pamphlet is about half done and I work on it when I have time. I showed a plate of page one to one of my students and he said that it was so simple that anyone could understand Igbo from it. I hope that he is right as far as Americans are concerned.

I'd like to wish you belated birthday greetings. Dottie only told me about your birthday recently.

We are in the midst of the rainy season and everything is lush and green.

Dottie and I are getting "end of tour-ish" which means that we spend much time speculating on what it will be like returning home to the temperate zone, big cities, restaurants, entertainment, etc. This is an amusement of infinite variety.

Sincerely,

Hershel

Letter of May 23, 1963

Dear Folks,

People are coming and going around here as usual, mostly going.

We went to Father McGlade's new church, which he built next to his borehole. It holds three thousand people. Now he has gone home to Ireland for leave, and quite possibly will not return to Africa. He says he wants to go to South America.

Within the next two weeks most of the Peace Corps group will have left. Then many of the university faculty; almost half are due to leave the end of June. They sign three-year contracts and they have been here since the beginning of the university, which is now three years old. So it is rather a milestone to have the original staff leaving. The students' clubs have a sort of ritual. They give receptions in the refectory, which can accommodate two receptions at the same time, so no one can hear what is going on at either one. The chairman is introduced, then his supporters, then dancing, then farewell addresses, which are mimeographed and distributed. These are very personal and unabashed comments as to how students feel about instructors. Then the instructors must respond, and more dancing and then closing remarks. This all takes place from 4:00 to 6:00 p.m. Receptions have been going on for two weeks and I suppose next week as well.

The Modern Language Association, which consists of students majoring in modern languages, gave a farewell reception for Hans Maitre (German instructor loaned by the German government who pays his salary) and Brigid Eyres (a volunteer with the British Graduate Volunteer Service Overseas) who teaches French to the majors. She lived in the dormitories with the Peace Corps women. She is paid only $6.00 a week for incidental expenses. We call her a British Peace Corps volunteer. And I was included. I taught French to the non-majors; I think there were about two hundred. I shall send copies of the address.

The day before, the Nigerian-America Friendship Society gave a reception for the Peace Corps. My 4:00 p.m. class has been empty all week with the receptions and other events going on.

I gave my classes a kind of mock exam, which I will hand back tomorrow (Friday). I am already beginning to feel end of job depression, which is worse than having a vacation. After working intensely for five months, it is a terrible drop. But then, you work all year without a vacation, don't you, Pop.

Love,
Dot

Letter of June 22, 1963

Dear Folks,

Commencement week was very exciting here. As the week went on from the baccalaureate services on Sunday to the final exercises on Saturday, the "graduates" got more and more excited. Class pictures with Zik and the vice chancellor in their gowns, class night exercises with speeches of members of the class who got first class honors degrees—very good speeches, outspoken and thoughtful, and wise! Then graduation rehearsal and finally Saturday, June 15 came!

The first graduates from the University of Nigeria—and in fact from the first indigenous university in Africa! All the rest have been founded by missionaries or colonialists and the degrees read "graduation from the University of London at Ibadan," etc. Not even now does Ibadan give its own degrees. It soon will. So this was really a tremendous moment for higher education in Africa.

Graduation procession

The guests included: The sardauna of Sokoto—the governor of the North and possibly the most powerful man in the country. The North by virtue of its population and size dominates Nigerian politics, although of course, not the economy. Nigeria's natural resources are mainly in the Eastern and Western Regions. Ibrahim is the elected governor of the North. The sardauna would be the traditional ruler. Ibrahim also received an honorary degree. Several powerful Lagos politicians, men of letters, and of course Zik. Okpara and Ibian, the heads of the Eastern government, received degrees. One little gal in the graduating class—Janet Elemo—gave a rousing speech on the rights of women, on behalf of the eleven girls in the class. She said that the University of Nigeria was the first institution of higher learning in Nigeria to be coeducational from the very beginning of its existence. She mentioned that even our sisters at Ibadan would not have degrees from an African university. It was very well done and would have thrilled you, mother.

The program was very long. Zik read telegrams from all over the world congratulating the university. These included ones from Ralph Bunche, Professor Rupert Emerson at Harvard, U Thant, the UN secretary-general, and the president of Howard University. Zik went there!

The day afterward some of the Peace Corps were driving to Kaduna and Kano to be interviewed for various things and to catch their planes at Kano. The car wasn't full so joined them. I had not seen the North at all so was thrilled at the chance!

We drove the first day to Jos. Jos is on a plateau and has the most delicious of climates in all of Nigeria! It has an enormous European population and is supposed to be sort of a resort. We had breakfast that morning at the Hill Station, which is rather like a beautifully cared for ski resort. It had wall-to-wall carpeting, huge lounges, huge upholstered armchairs, all rather overwhelming luxury and, I recall, hard to take. The drive to Jos was over very bad roads and fifty miles or so in a blinding rainstorm. So it is not something one does every day!

Then we went on to Kaduna, the capital of the Northern Region. We stayed at the Peace Corps rest house there. I stayed with other girls at the house of the new Peace Corps representative, Jack Wilmore. Saw a lot of Peace Corps volunteers I had not seen since leaving them in Lagos in December 1961!

We drove the next day to Kano. We learned that there was to be a Durbar on Thursday,—which was a real stroke of luck. A Durbar is a celebration of a holy war. Something like when the Igbos want to celebrate something, they put on a masquerade dance. It's a big parade with each district riding horseback to salute the emir. This was a celebration of the installation of a new emir of Kano. You can imagine what it would mean in a power structure of a Hausa-Fulani kingdom of a Muslim people. It seems feudalistic: the chiefs pay tithes to the emirs who pay tithes to the sardauna. Fascinating living portrayal of the Arabian nights!

We wandered around Kano market on Wednesday. The Hausa sit back in little mud booths selling all kinds of handicrafts. It is one of the biggest markets in West Africa. There are leather sandals, bags, embroidered cloth, hats, blankets, camel blankets, calabashes.

Finally Thursday morning came. We woke up at 4:00 a.m. to take one of the boys to the airport—he was flying to Lagos and then to Khartoum. We found five PCVs had arrived during the night and were stretched out in the patio of the house where we were staying. There were at least ten PCVs there the night we were! After putting Howard on the plane we picked up the rest of the group and went to the house of two PCVs for breakfast. Then we walked about one and a quarter miles to the stadium for the Durbar. The boys stood up on the wall but Brigid and I pushed our way into the stadium and found seats. We were only about thirty feet from the parade and could see everything.

First the dignitaries arrived, the provincial governor, etc. Each came in a swanky car more beautiful than the last one! Their colorful brigades of horses walked before and behind the limousines—Rolls-Royces, Cadillacs, Lincolns. Speeches were made which no one could even hear. Then the Durbar started. Some 2,000 horses paraded in, their riders arranged in groups representing each district in the Kano Emirate. The chiefs had to pay tribute to the new emir. Their costumes were breathtaking, mountainous turbans of blue-gold polished cloth, with flowing robes of silver or gold embroidered on rich blue or black cloth. Some seemed so heavily clothed, one could not imagine how the horses moved at all. Each group was preceded by musicians and dancers, and sometimes wrestlers. Only the children and young women dance in the North. After that the women are in purdah and the men become warriors or horsemen.

Then selected riders participated in the jaffi gallop and salute to the new emir. A group of horsemen would line up. They would maintain this line down the field. At a signal they gallop as fast as they can down the field, reining their hoses to a stop right under the emir's nose!! This was very exciting, with robes flying behind them, screaming as they went! The last jaffi was about thirty warriors. They held shields. With their robes and turbans flying, screaming, it was a very beautiful event!

We sent off our trunk and two footlockers last week to Hersh's brother in San Francisco. That is, we took things to Enugu and Jack Wilmore said they would go by AID car to Lagos. One of the footlockers is full of just curios, masks and things. We have still some masks and musical instruments to send.

We have five weeks left and with the university empty, Nsukka seems really desolate. What a conception it was to put a university way back in the bush here to begin with. Africa is truly fascinating.

Love,

Dot

Final Word

Rereading my letters and writing this book has given me a fresh appreciation of my two years in Nigeria. Those two years in the Peace Corps forever changed my life.

Besides having the insights and experiences of being a part of an emerging independent country, and getting married there, I have lived in California for the past fifty years and raised three remarkable children. I have had many opportunities to share my experiences in Nigeria in speeches to groups in the community, in my classes, and with family and friends.

Hershel has taught high school students for thirty-five years. He has taught about Nigeria and developed curriculum material for his school district. In 1983 he returned to Nigeria with a group organized by Stanford. They stayed in Northern Nigeria and were not allowed to visit the Eastern Region because it was thought to be too dangerous.

A group of PCVs returned to Nigeria a few years ago. They found that the railroad no longer runs, there are huge potholes in the roads, and schools where they taught have crumbled. Nigeria has not maintained its infrastructure. The group did not go out at night, as it was considered too dangerous. Nigeria has enormous wealth in natural resources, especially in oil, and though the population has more than doubled since I was there—it is now over one hundred million—the members of the wealthy class and the politicians are the ones who profit.

I recently read *Americanah*, a novel by Chimamanda Ngozi Adichie. It describes graduates of the University of Nigeria, Nsukka during the past decade. All of them plan to lead their lives in England or America. The main character, Ifemelu, struggles with adapting to life in America. Their ties to Nigerian family and classmates remain strong, but they do not want to live in Nigeria. It makes me feel sad that Nigeria is losing its graduates.

During the Biafran War, 1967–70, Father McGlade organized Holy Ghost priests and others, some Peace Corps volunteers, to feed the people of Biafra and get as many children out as possible. He wrote me letters describing what was happening. I hope to write about this. Subsequently both the Holy Ghost fathers and the Peace Corps were thrown out of Nigeria, forbidden to return. The government felt their efforts had prolonged the war.

It was a privilege to be part of Nigeria's first years as an independent nation. Democracy is hard work. Each country must find its own way.

I hope I gave back to Nigeria as much as Nigeria gave to me. To quote Heraclitus: "Nothing ever is, everything is becoming."

A FAREWELL ADDRESS PRESENTED TO MRS D. HERZBERG ON THE OCCASION OF HER DEPARTURE FROM THE UNIVERSITY OF NIGERIA, NSUKKA

Dear Madam,

Mrs. D. Herzberg is a member of the American Peace Corps. She lectures in French and has been with us for two sessions. During this period she has shown a keen interest in her subject and a sense of co-operation. She has shown that she can work. She is highly principled, very strict in marking papers and awarding marks. Her students complain of heavy assignments and strict correction of their papers, but this has inspired them rather than discourage them. They have come to realise at last that the whole aim is directed towards achieving a general good and reaching a high standard. We are proud to say that this goal has been achieved. They are proud of your work and their standard can compare favourably with any student of their rank from any University.

Mrs. Herzberg is charming and well-behaved, always ready to respond to our daily greetings.

The work of the Peace Corps can no longer be over exaggerated. We hope that in the States you will be our gospel and encourage more Peace Corps especially those who can teach any of the languages we study here. We feel your loss greatly realising the difficulty of getting lecturers in the department of Modern languages.

We pray the Almighty to grant you and your husband long life and prosperity.

Accept this as a token for your good services.

We remain Madam,
For the Students of Modern Languages Association, University of Nigeria, Nsukka.

J.C. Iwudibiah,
President.

V.N. Ezechukwu,
Secretary.

U. Edebiri,
Ex-Officio.

19th May, 1963.

FAREWELL ADDRESS PRESENTED TO MEMBERS OF THE PEACE CORPS ON THE OCCASION OF A SEND-OFF PARTY ARRANGED FOR THEM BY MEMBERS OF THE NIGERIAN/AMERICAN FRIENDSHIP SOCIETY, UNIVERSITY OF NIGERIA, NSUKKA. 18th OF MAY, 1963

The chairman, the worthy representative members of the Peace Corps of the United States of America, representatives of the United States Information Service, Nigeria, ladies and gentlemen: Almost two years ago, we happily received within our fold, President Kennedy's "messengers of peace and goodwill," the Peace Corps. Today we are gathered here, with mixed feelings of happiness and sorrow, to say good-bye to the first batch of the Peace Corps who have honestly, conscientiously, untiringly, and selflessly dedicated their lives to the building of the University of Nigeria, Nsukka to an enviable position which this young institution of higher learning holds in the academic world today.

We would like to make it clear to those who are connected with the University of Nigeria, and to the Nigerian accommodating citizens, that the Peace Corps is an organization of several groups of young Americans who have indicated their enthusiasm in the progress of developing nations. As the chancellor of the University of Nigeria, the Rt. Hon. Dr. Nnamidi Azikiwe, has said, some of them, "come from families with a rich tradition and historical background. Some come from ancestors whose history is one of revolt and sacrifice against injustice and all forms of man's inhumanity to man. Some are descended from families, which lost one or more of their offspring in the fight against slavery of the African. Whilst some of them have come from different walks of life, full of enthusiasm to pass on their knowledge, no matter how meagre, to their fellow human beings across the Atlantic. Theirs is a labour of love; a spirit and desire of cooperation."

We do realize that the aims and purpose of the Peace Corps is reminiscent of the aims of the founders, of the first thirteen colonies of the United States of America. We are very intimate with the protracted and ultimate triumph of the 1776 struggle for independence.

We are aware that this struggle for American independence was not an affair to be limited to the territorial boundaries of the United States. This struggle has become a guiding star to other colonies, which, for a long time have been suffering under the heavy yoke of imperialism. In short, the American Declaration of Independence has become a classical inspiration for all freedom-loving peoples of the free world.

Ladies and gentlemen, let us remind you, that even before the Peace Corps philosophy was muted by the presentable President Kennedy, American statesmen, journalists, lawyers, doctors did in their nationalistic and humanitarian way contribute towards the constitutional development of Nigeria. A little thought will throw our reflection to the Atlantic Charter, signed by Prime Minister Churchill and President Roosevelt at Placentia Bay in Newfoundland on August 9, 1941. Ever since then, men like Wendell Willkie, Cordell Hull, Raymond Leslie Buell, and a host of other American personalities have fought to see that the third clause of the Atlantic Charter, which respects "the right of all peoples to choose the form of government under which they will live," has been practically carried out.

As a result of this, a new era has descended slowly upon the nations of the world. Joseph Palmer II, the United States ambassador to Nigeria, remarked that "We live in a world system that is based on concepts of the independence and freedom of nations. When the realization of these concepts break down and independence and freedom are lost or threatened, the entire international structure is affected. The genuine independence of each and every nation within the framework of the United Nations, the genuine freedom of peoples, and genuine progress towards economic and social development are therefore the best guarantees of the security, stability, and well-being of all states."

Nigeria is a nation on the run to economic maturity and social rehabilitation. This jet-propelled desire to meet up the more advanced countries of the world at a very reasonable time, demands of Nigeria, the training of her citizens in all the paraphernalia of learning to take up the responsibility of nation building. Nigeria cannot do this in isolation. Hence we have found the work of the Peace Corps of valuable significance at this present stage of Nigeria's development.

These members of the Peace Corps have been with us for more than a year now. We have had the opportunity to study their historical background and appreciate their abilities as friends, individuals, fellow human beings, and teachers; they have given us the best in them. They have also learned much from Nigerians. No human being is unalloyed in character par excellence. Therefore, we shall be failing in our mature and sane judgment, if for the lapse of one or two individuals, we condemn these "messengers of peace and goodwill." We wanted the services of those who know, because we are thirsty for genuine knowledge.

The members of the Peace Corps have given us much of this knowledge.

Mr. Chairman, before the final word, we would wish to express our regret about the recent racial disturbances in Alabama. We know that the United States Constitution admits Negroes to full citizenship and guarantees constitutional protection, for their rights and liberties, forbidding incrimination against them because of race, color, creed, or previous condition of servitude. We are therefore noting with regret and pain, that while sincere efforts are being made to uphold this provision of Negroes rights in the United States Constitution, the bulk of the southern part of that country is unashamedly indulging in the brutal and unholy practice of race prejudice by still discriminating against peoples of black colour. In spite of these setbacks practised by some of the racists of the southern United States, we still recognise that the United States remains the beacon of an ideal—the ideal of human equality, liberty, and institutional expression, of the dignity and sanctity of the human personality and of the inalienable rights of man.

We hope that the present members of the departing Peace Corps will act as a lubrication between the Negroes and whites in the United States. We hope you will revive and maintain the philosophy of the drafters of the United States Constitution, which states, "... We ... hold these truths to be self-evident, that all men are created equal, that they are endowed by their creator with certain unalienable rights, that among these are life, liberty, and the pursuit of happiness ..."

But, the members of the Peace Corps should have no misconception about our views towards them. Our conception about you is high. We regard you as men and women of high integrity, courage, and devotion. Further, our thanks to you would be manifold if you can only make many of the Americans know what we are, who we are, and whom we are. We need further exchanges of this nature. We are still to know more of ourselves. We however regret that at the moment our society has not been able to arrange exchange programs; but we are optimistic that in the near future this important aspect of the society's objectives will be put to play and therein increase awareness between the peoples of Nigeria and America, the aspirations and problems of each other.

In conclusion, we express our gratitude to the director of the Peace Corps, Mr. Shriver, who has made it possible for the University of Nigeria—and Nigeria in general—to share the United States educational program for the less developed countries.

We have lived together for almost twenty-four months. We have learned much from you. We have taken much of your philosophy, your dynamism, and your sincere approach to pressing world issues. We hope we shall still drink of this free gift from the next batch of Peace Corps. The much you have learned from us, we hope you will hold willingly and without colouration.

This woman was considered to be the oldest in the village
of Nsukka Station based on the breadth of her memory alone,
because there were no birth records as we know them

Student Essays

"Nsukka" by Stephen Ugwu

Nsukka Station is a small village in Eastern Nigeria and Nsukka Division. It is populated by the Igbo tribe. Nsukka Station is bounded in the North by Obukpa, in the South by Lejia, in the West by Edem-Ani, and in the East by Orba. Nsukka is known all the world over because of its salubrious climate, and because it is the site of the University of Nigeria. It lies between the savanna and deciduous forests. Nsukka has no mountains but is surrounded by many small hills. Among the common trees that are found in Nsukka are the Iroko and the Mango. Nsukka has two major seasons a year, the dry and the rainy season. Every year during the height of the dry season a strong wind blows from the Sahara and makes the Nsukka quite cold and dry. This wind is called the Harmattan. When this wind is blowing Nsukka is so cold that many people find it too uncomfortable to bathe. Europeans rush to live in Nsukka because its climate suits them. There is no river in this village. This village has a population of roughly 12,000 inhabitants. There are markets in Nsukka, about four in number, which correspond to the four-day native week.

Every area has its own customs. In many places women do plant crops, but in Nsukka it is the last thing a woman would do. The custom at Nsukka is that if the husband of a woman has died, the woman has to be in her husband's compound for a year and then she becomes part of his brother's family. The usual dress of women is a long piece of cloth called "the wrapper." The main occupations for women are cooking and trading. Trading in yams is the most popular. It is the custom here that a man is entitled to sit down before the women. Old people in Nsukka are very much respected and when a man reaches a certain age he very often will take a title. The name of one title is Oziooko.

The principal foods are yams, cassava, and sweet potatoes. The land here is very productive for these crops, people here use crop rotation also. Nsukka is noted for its production of palm wine, so it is quite obvious that the people drink plenty of it. Palm oil is also found here in abundance and is very delicious. It is used to make soup. Formerly they used their hands to eat but now things have changed and utensils are used. Wrestling, music, and dancing are the chief forms of entertainment. Many of the houses are built of mud with grass roofs, but newer houses have tin or aluminum roofs. Material and spiritual well-being are increasing in Nsukka.

* * *

"Eha-Amufu" by Pertrand Ewelum

Eha-Amufu is a small village in the Nsukka division. It is situated in the northern part of eastern Nigeria. The village is fairly small and is composed of different tribes. Though there are more Igbos, there are also people of the Yoruba, Fulani, Hausa, and Ijaw tribes. The Hausas form one-fifth of the whole population because the village is very close to the northern region of Kigeria. The climate of Eha-Amufu is moderately hot. A river runs through the village. Though the river is not fit for drinking, many people drink from it.

The population of Eha-Amufu is roughly 8,000. The size of the village is about three square miles. The people are chiefly noted for their economy. They do not spend much and they do not gain much. Their main occupations are farming and fishing. The women of Eha-Amufu usually have some occupation other than child care and being a housewife. The people of Eha-Amufu have their own customs just as other villages. For them, customs are laws. Their main foods are yams, cassava, garri, potatoes, beans, as well as assorted native greens. Their utensils are mortars, pestles, pots, knives, and bowls.

The people of Eha-Amufu live in a community. There are many churches, which serve the many tribes. Some of the churches are: Catholic, Muslim, Pagan, and Church Missionary Society of England.

Eha-Amufu is important because it has the only railway station in Nsukka Division. Its big market and lumber industry are also very important for the lives of the people.

* * *

"Anambra" by Thomas Eche

Our village is named after the river Anambra, which runs nearby and then into the Niger. It is located near the town of Onitsha, which is the largest trading center in Nigeria. The inhabitants of this village are all Igbo. The average temperature in this village is 70 degrees and it is surrounded by forests of tall trees. Rain falls in abundance for about six months of the year.

The main occupations of our villagers are farming, trading, and fishing. The people live in large families, which are called Ododu. Thousands of people live in our village.

One of the customs of our village is that if a stranger comes to a person's house it is compulsory that his hand be shaken and that he be given kola. Kola is a nut which symbolizes friendship. Another custom is that juniors must always show respect to seniors.

Our foods are mainly yam, rice, cassava, cocoyam, beans, and potatoes. Our utensils consist of mortars, pestles, clay pots, Igbo plates made of wood, and baskets, which are made out of parts of the palm tree. The most important activity of the villagers is going to market where they trade and talk with their friends. Palm wine is also an activity.

* * *

"Addazi" by Michael Okaiah

Addazi is a village in Owerri Province. It has an equatorial climate. It is about twenty square miles and has a population of 5,000 inhabitants. Villagers in Addazi build their huts out of mud, and each hut has a characteristic spire where the thatch comes to a point. Goats are tethered to the huts and hens are usually found running around them. There is only one very tiny general store in this town. The population has two religions, the older pagan and the newer Catholic religion. There is a church, which has a tower that shows above the trees and the church bell can be heard quite clearly in the village. Inhabitants of the village have many occupations such as farming, hunting, fishing, carpentry, and teaching

As they are mostly farmers, they have plenty to eat such as yam, cassava, rice, cocoyam, and plantain. In nearby Ugu they find fish in abundance. Some even have houseboats and sail about the lake in search of food and adventure. Hunters also stay away from the village in the forest, killing and then selling their game in distant villages. Sometimes the hunters stay away for weeks.

During the day the men go out to work, the boys go to school, and the girls help their mothers at home.

* * *

Newspaper Clippings

THE REPORTER DISPATCH, WHITE PLAINS, N.Y., FRIDAY, SEPTEMBER 21, 1962

Scarsdalian To Teach At Nsukka U.

SCARSDALE—
Nsukka University in Nigeria will have as one of its new teachers this fall the former Miss Dorothy L. Crews, daughter of Mr. and Mrs. Floyd H. Crews, of 19 Montrose Road. Married last May to fellow Peace Corps volunteer, Hershel Z. Herzberg of San Francisco and New York, Mrs. Herzberg taught first at the only government secondary school for girls in Eastern Nigeria, located in Enugu, the capital city.

After her marriage she was transferred to St. Teresa's College in Nsukka, a secondary school for boys where her husband also has been teaching.

Mrs. Herzberg is a graduate of Scarsdale High School and Pembroke College and has an M.A. degree in history from Stanford University. She had experience in social service work and as a teacher in private schools before joining the Peace Corps. She has traveled extensively and speaks several languages.

Mrs. Herzberg, who went to Nigeria with the first group of Peace Corps volunteers who were trained at Harvard University, is a graduate of University of California in Berkeley, a former law school student and high school teacher.

TUESDAY, SEPTEMBER 11, 1962 — WEST AFRICAN PILOT

'Operation Book Shelf'

ENUGU, Sept. 10.—An American organisation known as "Operation Book Shelf" sponsored by Scarsdale Women's Club, Scarsdale, New York, has sent 1,024 books worth about £800 to Miss Dottie Crews Herzberg of Queen's School here.

Miss Herzberg, a Peace Corps volunteer, who hails from Scarsdale, told newsmen that "Operation Book Shelf" was a voluntary agency founded in 1954.

It had already distributed freely more than 132,000 volumes of books to libraries in and outside the United States, she disclosed.

152   Me, Madam

THE REPORTER DISPATCH

WHITE PLAINS, N.Y., TUESDAY, DECEMBER 26, 1961

Scarsdale Woman, Peace Corps Member, Sees 'No Better Way to Serve Country'

By RICHARD F. GRIFFIN

SCARSDALE—

The Peace Corps and Nigeria may be just words to many people, but for Dorothy L. Crews, they will play an important part in her life for the next two years.

Miss Crews, the daughter of Mr. and Mrs. Floyd Crews, 19 Montrose Road, will be embarking Wednesday along with 43 members of a Peace Corps contingent which will teach and assist the Nigerians to develop their country.

For this attractive young lady of 26, it is not the first adventure of this sort, but another chapter in existance which has taken her from Providence, R.I., where she did settlement house work while a student at Pembroke-Brown University to a tiny village work camp in Nativitas, south of Mexico City, where she was a recreation director for Mexican children.

Upon her return to the United States, Miss Crews continued her studies at Leland Stanford University, gaining an M.A. in history and in the meantime continuing her settlement work in San Francisco.

Upon graduation from college, Miss Crews worked for Little, Brown and Co. Boston, as a secretary, and then she taught the sixth grade in an elementary school in New Haven, Conn.

Went to Copenhagen

The spirit of adventure, which has also taken Miss Crews to Copenhagen, Denmark, is not her main reason for going to Nigeria, but, as she says, "It is the best way that I can use the skills I have acquired, and I can see no better way to serve my country than aiding in the development of this country (Nigeria)."

"The group I am going with," Miss Crews went on to say, "is well trained in all areas necessary to assist the people of Nigeria."

Miss Crews, who says she believes she is the only Westchester resident accepted so far for Peace Corps work, says she feels the preliminary training at the University of California at Los Angeles prepared her and her group well for the tasks they are to perform with the Corps.

While at UCLA, Miss Crews went on to say, "we were given a very extensive program in the area of African culture, which gave us a clear insight as to native customs and habits." "Aiding us a great deal in our work were several students from Nigeria who, understanding the work we will be doing, gave us first-hand knowledge of their country."

"Student teaching in the high schools of Los Angeles was a very enjoyable experience" remarked Miss Crews, who taught both English and History.

Miss Crew, besides her various accomplishments, is also an accomplished guitar player.

For a girl who always had the "yen" for travel, lectures at UCLA on African History created a desire for her future assignment. The lectures were only a part of the 60 hours of lectures a week that the group attended.

Physical Training Given

Besides the academic training that the group went through, tropical medicine was part of the training.

An interesting but important part of the training Miss Crews said, was the physical education training in which the candidates learned the various sports native to the area of their assignment. Culminating the physical training was a soccer game between the Peace Corps trainees and the Nigerian students, the outcome of which Miss Crews would not divulge.

PEACE CORPS member Dorothy Crews, 19 Montrose Road, Scarsdale, points out her corps assignments in Nigeria to her mother, Mrs. Floyd H. Crews. Miss Crews leaves for her tour with the corps on Wednesday. Staff Photo by Steve Gonda.

Looking forward with enthusiasm towards her arrival in Lagos, the Nigerian capital, next week, and her possible assignment in the Enugu area, Miss Crews said she feels that her teaching of the Nigerians and living near them in a school compound will be an enriching experience.

Asked how she expects to spend her vacations, Miss Crews said, "The Corps will hold seminars for the group in Lagos, where we will be able to exchange our varying experience."

Asked what her future plans were, Miss Crews remarked, "I will probably sign up for another tour with the Corps. Even if I don't the experience I have obtained will make me a better teacher when I returne home."

PEMBROKERS SERVING

As PUBLIC ENTHUSIASM for the Peace Corps continues to grow, so does the number of Pembrokers among these volunteers. They enlarge the group of alumnae already serving overseas, some with many years' experience, as government employees, teachers, or missionaries. *Pembroke Alumna* asked several of these alumnae to tell us something about what they are doing and what they hope to accomplish.

The Peace Corps

Additions to the list of Pembroke volunteers for the Peace Corps have come frequently in recent months. Among those serving are **Estelle Freeman Harris '36** and her husband, Walter D. Harris '35, and **Roberta Quarles '60**, teaching in Ethiopia; **Barbara Crumbaker '60**, teaching in the Philippines; **Rosalind Pace Pearson '60** and her husband, Robert '60, teaching in Afghanistan; and **Helene G. Lew '62**, serving in North Borneo.

Letters from another Peace Corps volunteer, **Barbara Fontaine '58**, who is teaching chemistry and physics in Addis Ababa, Ethiopia, inspired the substitution of donations to her school for the traditional small presents at the John Hay Library Christmas party.

Representing Pembroke alumnae in the Peace Corps in this article are **Elizabeth Kreusler Ehmann '55**, who, with her husband, Carl '56, are in their second year of teaching in Sierra Leone, and **Dorothy Crews Herzberg '57**, who has been teaching in Nigeria for the past year and married another volunteer last May.

Experiences in an American Friends Service Committee work camp in Mexico, in Herald Tribune Fresh Air Fund Camps in the Catskills, and in Brown Youth Guidance and Scouting had already given **Dorothy Crews Herzberg** new insights and perspectives. "I was immediately captured by the idea of young Americans working in the villages of Asia, Africa, and South America when it was first proposed," she writes. "Nothing can replace the enrichment of living and working daily with peoples of another culture—and this I knew would be one of the richest rewards such a government-sponsored program would give."

Now teaching French at the University of Nigeria in Nsukka, Dorothy's experience in the Peace Corps has been somewhat unusual because of her marriage to another volunteer she met overseas. She first taught English and history at Queens School, a government secondary school for girls in eastern Nigeria, where she also worked with the Folk Dancing Society and developed a small chorus of girls. After her marriage last May to Hershel Herzberg, another Peace Corps volunteer, she taught mathematics at St. Teresa's Secondary School for boys in Nsukka, where her husband was teaching. There she started a chorus of boys which she still works with, though no longer on St. Teresa's staff. In the villages around Nsukka, Dorothy has developed sewing projects with 30 to 40 little girls. Girls who can sew, she notes, can ask a higher dowry price and thus expect better husbands. Working with boys and girls in Africa has also enriched and broadened her understanding of teenagers: "They have the same problems anywhere!"

154 Me, Madam

THE REPORTER DISPATCH, WHITE PLAINS, N.Y., WEDNESDAY, JUNE 20, 1962

Books for Africa

ANOTHER LOAD of books is now on the high seas, this one en route to Egunu, East Nigeria to assist the teaching work of Miss Dorothy Crews of Scarsdale. Operation Bookshelf, through the combined efforts of many civic, youth and other volunteer groups, the Scarsdale Womans Club and the Harvey Birch chapter of the Daughters of the American Revolution, has made it possible for 1,750 lbs. of educational books to be shipped. Shown at the dock are, left to right, James Noble Jr., whose company Noble Van and Storage Co. contributed transportation to the boat; Mrs. Donald F. Sealy, chairman of Operation Bookshelf; Mrs. Gibson M. Allen, regent of the Harvey Birch DAR who is presenting a check for the cost of shipping the cargo to Mrs. Sealy and Mrs. Russell M. Skelton, immediate past regent, all of Scarsdale.

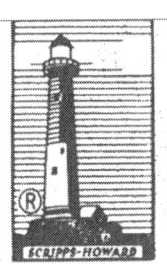

New York World-Telegram
The Sun

A SCRIPPS-HOWARD NEWSPAPER

RICHARD D. PETERS, Editor MATT MEYER, Business Manager
LEE B. WOOD, President

PAGE 22   Thursday, Sept. 27, 1962

By Robert C. Ruark

Leave the Peace Corps Alone!

As is usual with election years, no dead cat will be left unflung, no skeleton unrattled, but I think that one of the things the politicians might well leave alone is the Peace Corps. By all accounts, it's done a whale of a job in the manner intended, and I don't think it should be lint-picked to pieces.

Nobody was more dedicatedly against the Peace Corps when it was first announced than your correspondent. I smote it hip-and-thigh in at least a half-dozen pieces.

There are still certain things about its burgeoning budget that might stand question, and one is the very serious future consideration of what is to be done by the government about service-incurred disabilities.

But largely wherever I've been in the world over the last six months—and my worst enemy can't accuse me of immobility—all I've heard is praise for the Peace Corps' solid, helpful work and generally fine projection of the best American image with the downtrods.

Perhaps the actual performance means nothing very much in the sum, but the advertising is great for our country. And folk-dancing seems to have been downheld to a minimum.

* * *

You never heard very much of good about what we used to call "Pointless Four" people and, of course, the diplomats always come in for a knock from the locals. The typical American abroad, including a lot of backwater military service personnel with service wives and ill-raised kids and car pools and supermarket PXs, riled the natives.

Our junketing Congressmen, notably the likes of the Rev. Adam Clayton Powell, shrink us in the estimation of the people we try to impress with apple-pie American heart and soul.

But the Peace Corps kids have worked well at what it was announced that they would accomplish—a better knowledge of the foreign lands and the natives for themselves, whilst bestowing some added know-how and inspiration to the local camel-wallahs and yak-tenders.

* * *

There have been a few embarrassing incidents, such as the rumpus raised over the poor girl who penned a postcard saying that there was the odd pig in the muddy streets and chickens roosted on the bedstead in West Africa; that, in short, things were not all Waldorf with the plumbing and every night was not a jam session.

It was a normal postcard like one from nearly any place that tourists travel, and there must have been a few million acid commentaries on the mercenary quotient of the French and the lack of ice water in England this past summer.

There was a stupid administrative error in a ticklish and criticism-susceptible organization when a $10,000-a-year career worker—not a volunteer—received travel allowances for a wife and nine children to go to the Philippines. That tab, considering return trip, reaches the round sum of $26,380, and somebody should have known that Louisiana's Rep. Otto Passman, a friend for reduction in foreign aid who also happens to be chairman of the foreign operations subcommittee, would leap on it with gleefully anguished cries.

* * *

Those things happen, and will happen, and cost no more than a solid Folies Bergere-Pyramid viewing trip for a junketing Congressman and his or somebody else's wife.

Apart from a few goofs such as the above, I'd say that Sargent Shriver, who labors under the handicap of being the President's brother-in-law, has done a stout job and should be commended. He certainly has performed a noble feat of defending his baby from the professional wolves in Congress and the ravening bears, such as myself, of the syndicated typewriter pack.

There'll be enough political throats to cut this year and I think that the Peace Corps should be let alone. It's the only thing in the Kennedy administration so far that seems to have worked.

NEW YORK Herald Tribune

Wednesday, October 3, 1962

As the Peace Corps Stands Now

In the Cause of Freedom

Peace Corps volunteers are free and independent agents, Sargent Shriver, director of the Corps, said yesterday. They sign up for two years, but can quit at any time. "We remind them of that," he said, "and it is one of the best ways of stopping complaints."

"Once they are in the field," he continued, "we don't tell them what to do. They are not under our immediate supervision—they are free to work things out for themselves. As I have told them, they can even read the New York Herald Tribune!"

asked whether they want to serve another tour, he said, and governments are being asked if they wish to keep the same volunteers or get new ones.

At a press conference in the Foreign Correspondents Center, 340 E. 46th St., Mr. Shriver answered a variety of questions, ranging from finance to romance.

He said the first 18 months of the Peace Corps had shown the basic need for "human skills" in economic development. "Without skilled men and women, economic development will not take place," he stated.

Mr. Shriver discussed the international conference on the development of human skills, to be held in Puerto Rico on Oct. 10-12, under the sponsorship of the Peace Corps. Delegates of more than 40 nations—both developed and developing—will attend.

"The conference may have the effect of changing the focus of international development," he said—with less emphasis on money and more on human skills.

Mr. Shriver said there are 4,000 Peace Corps volunteers working, or ready for work, in 43 nations. Next year, there will be 10,000 volunteers in 50 countries. The Peace Corps is not a "youth organization," he said, with 300 members over 50 and six over 70.

"The drop out rate has been very low, surprising every one, including myself," he said. "Out of the first 2,500 we lost only 25—two by death in planes. Only 10 or 12 volunteers really failed to adjust."

On finance, he said it costs $9,000 to train, transport and maintain a volunteer. Wages range from $60 to $180 a month, depending upon living costs in the host country, permitting volunteers to live "comfortably but not luxuriously." Although they are not asked to do so, every host country has provided funds or equipment to help the Corpsmen.

On romance, he said the Peace Corps discouraged marriage during the term of service, but 15 workers have been married—to fellow volunteers, or to citizens of the lands where they are working.

New York's

Arrests for major crimes first six months of 1962, State Paul D. McGinnis said today.

The commissioner said t first half of the year was 3.8 15,643 arrests from April th quarterly total on record.

All sections of the state co the commissioner said, except

He said the Correction D cessed 19,708 reports during arrests for major crimes. H convictions.

Mr. McGinnis said the ocured in arrests for gambling, ful entry. He said arrests ir recorded a sizable decline.

The narcotics arrest decli group. Arrests of youths 16 t charges rose 6.6 per cent.

PEACE CORPS VOLUNTEER

December 1962, Vol. 1, No. 2

ONE THOUSAND BOOKS, donated in the United States, are unpacked on arrival at Queen's School, Enugu, Nigeria, by Volunteer Dorothy Herzberg (Scarsdale, N. Y.) and friends. The books, collected by the Scarsdale Women's Club and shipped to Nigeria by a chapter of the Daughters of the American Revolution, will be shared with St. Teresa's College, a library, and rural schools.

List of Letters and Student Essays

Letter of January 4, 1962	14
Letter of January 9, 1962	16
Letter of January 12, 1962	18
Letter of January 19, 1962	25
Letter of January 25, 1962, Edward R. Murrow	26
Letter of February 12, 1962	28
Letter of February 17, 1962	30
Letter of February 24, 1962	31
Letter of March 4, 1962	31
Letter of March 20, 1962	32
Letter of March 28, 1962	34
Letter of April 10, 1962	35
Letter of May 2, 1962	36
Letter of May 14, 1962	39
Letter of May 31, 1962	41
Letter from Hershel of June 8, 1962	48
Letter of June 10, 1962	49
Letter of June 11, 1962	50
Letter of June 16, 1962	52
Letter of June 24, 1962	54
Letter of July 5, 1962	57
Letter of July 10, 1962	57
Letter of July 16, 1962, Father McGlade	61
Letter of July 20, 1962	66
Letter of July 31, 1962	66
Letter from Hershel of July 31, 1962	68
Letter of August 13, 1962	69
Letter of August 19, 1962	71
Letter of August 31, 1962	73
Letter of September 1, 1962, Books Arrive	74
Letter of September 1,6,12,22, 1962, Sewing Projecs	76
In a Little Newsletter Called *The Tille Lamp*	77
Letter of November 1, 1962	77
Letter of November 8, 1962	78
Letter of November 17, 1962	78
Letter of November 28, 1962	79
Letter of September 16, 1962	84

List of Letters and Student Essays 159

Letter of September 27, 1962	85
Letter of September 30, 1962	86
Letter of October 4, 1962	87
Letter of October 21, 1962	89
Letter of October 26, 1962	90
Letter of November 1, 1962, Student Strike	92
Letter of November 3, 1962	94
Letter of November 7, 1962, Resolution of Riots	95
Letter of November 8, 1962	96
Letter of November 13, 1962	96
Letter of November 22, 1962	98
Letter of December 7, 1962	99
Letter of December 13, 1962	100
Letter of January 9, 1963	101
Letter from Hershel of January 14, 1963	104
Letter of January 15, 1963	106
Letter of January 25, 1963	107
Letter of February 1, 1963	114
Letter from Hershel of February 19, 1963	116
Letter of February 19, 1963	118
Letter of February 24, 1963	118
Letter of March 3, 1963	119
Letter of March 8, 1963	120
Letter of March 14, 1953	121
Letter from Hershel of March 15, 1963	121
Letter of April 4, 1963	123
Letter of April 10, 1963	126
Letter of April 15, 1963	128
Letter of April 19, 1963	129
Letter of May 3, 1963	130
Letter from Hershel of May 5, 1963	131
Letter of May 23, 1963	132
Letter of June 22, 1963	134
Farewell Address	142
"Nsukka" by Stephen Ugwu	147
"Eha-Amufu" by Pertrand Ewelum	148
"Anambra" by Thomas Eche	149
"Addazi" by Michael Okaiah	150

From back cover: Dorothy with Sargent Shriver in Washington, DC for the thirtieth Peace Corps reunion, August 1991

About the Author

Dorothy Crews Herzberg lives in the San Francisco Bay Area with her husband, Douglas Frew. She is an author, teacher, and mother of three, with four grandchildren. Retired after fourteen years of teaching English as a second language in the West Contra Costa School District.

In 2010 Dorothy was named *El Cerrito Woman of the Year* and received the *Jefferson Award for Public Service*. Between 2001 and 2012 she raised $300,000 and brought two hundred students and twenty-two teachers from Kennedy High School in Richmond to Washington, DC. There they participated in the Close Up Foundation's program, for an inside look at democracy in action. She currently serves on three community boards, and continues to substitute teach in Bay Area high schools.

Dorothy would love to hear you comments. You can email her at dorothyherzberg@gmail.com